Advanced Longsword

FORM AND FUNCTION

This work was brought to you by
The School of European Swordsmanship
www.swordschool.com
And the patrons of this work,
who donated either directly or through Indiegogo.

ISBN 978-952-7157-07-7 (hardback)
ISBN 978-952-7157-06-0 (paperback)
ISBN 978-952-7157-04-6 (PDF)
ISBN 978-952-7157-03-9 (EPUB)
ISBN 978-952-7157-05-3 (MOBI)

Book Design by Zebedee Design & Typesetting Services
(www.zebedeedesign.co.uk)

Printed by Lightning Source

MASTERING THE ART OF ARMS

Volume 3

Advanced Longsword

FORM AND FUNCTION

Guy Windsor

For Jaana and Orava, who have supported me, my School, and the Art of Arms in a million different ways over the last fifteen years. "Thank you" doesn't quite cover it.

CONTENTS

INTRODUCTION TO THE MASTERING THE ART OF ARMS COLLECTION

In late 2009 I set out to write a longsword training manual to replace my first book, *The Swordsman's Companion*, which was finished in 2003 and published in 2004. Around that time, I had moved away from training and teaching Fiore's longsword material in isolation from the rest of the system, and we have routinely incorporated the dagger material into our "longsword classes" since then. Naturally I wanted to put a chapter on falling and dagger basics into my new book, which was ready in its first draft by mid-2011, but it was clearly getting too big for a single volume. So I cut out the one long-ish chapter on the dagger and some of the footwork and falling material, and then played around with the idea of making a separate dagger book. This was clearly a good idea, because the book was written a week later. Round about the same time it became apparent that the longsword book was still too big, so I carved off another volume, separating out the more advanced techniques.

While writing the dagger book, I wanted to point out that Fiore's original treatise was written in verse, and so I took a small chunk of his text and laid it out as such: the rhyming scheme became immediately apparent. I took the English translation and worked it into a sonnet; this spawned yet another volume, my *Armizare Vade Mecum* collection of mnemonic rhymes, published in November 2011.

What started as one book is now four. I want the books in the series (and who knows how many books will ultimately belong here: I'm working on a rapier primer and a falchion book as this goes to press) to work as stand-alone volumes, which necessitates some repetition of key actions and terminology. I have usually just copied sections such as "The Four Steps" from one book to another, pictures and all. In this Advanced longsword book I have assumed that you have a thorough knowledge of *The Medieval Longsword*, so that the basics of the style are clear in your mind before we look at the really sophisticated material.

Given that *The Medieval Longsword* ends with freeplay, it may seem odd that we are looking at form and technique again in this book. This is because once you have developed your core under-standing of the Art to the point that freeplay is a useful training tool (as opposed to simply fun), you are ready to go deep into the underlying structure. Without diagnostic tools, research and devel-opment grinds to a halt; you will be using this material to add both breadth and depth, and testing everything in pair drills, pressure drills and freeplay. There is just no point trying to teach (for example) the *punta falsa* to a student who is still having difficulty distinguishing between *fendenti* and *mezani*, or who has difficulty holding a five-step fencing sequence in their head. I urge you to read and practise the content of *The Medieval Longsword* before you attempt this material.

"There's a feeling of power in reserve, a power that drives right through the bone, like the shiver you sense in the shaft of an axe when you take it into your hand. You can strike, or you can not strike, and if you choose to hold back the blow, you can still feel inside you the resonance of the omitted thing."

Hilary Mantel, Wolf Hall

INTRODUCTION

Advanced technique is basic technique done really well. It's faster, harder, more efficient and more perfectly adapted to circumstances. This applies to the execution of a simple attack as much as it does to the ability to string a series of simple actions together into longer combinations. This book is designed to take the basic techniques and concepts put forth in the previous book and give you the tools to develop them to a pitch of practical and artistic excellence.

The difficulty in writing this book lay in organising it into a coherent structure: in taking my intuitive grasp of the material and setting it out into one coherent narrative. This has *always* been the difficulty, and I have no doubt that Fiore faced the same problem (if you don't know who Fiore is, set this book down and read *The Medieval Longsword*. Unlike all my other works to date, this text is not a standalone book but depends on you having already established a common frame of reference with me), though his intentions in writing his book were clearly different to mine. He set out to describe the Art as he understood it, never imagining that there might be readers who had not grown up with the sword. I am trying to make my understanding of his Art accessible to modern practitioners.

Then it struck me. The mechanism we use for creating a narrative of the system within my students' brains is our "Syllabus Form" and, to a lesser extent, our "Cutting Drill". So I have arranged this book as an in-depth analysis of the steps of these drills. You can think of a form as a string of pearls. In the beginning, each pearl is just one technique or action. It's a tiny little seed pearl. But with practise, and a broadening understanding of the Art, each pearl becomes the locus for other concepts and actions to be stored. A single action acts as a trigger for a cascade of other things. So we begin with the Cutting Drill, which is a short form based on our four core drills: First Drill (*rebattere*

1

from the right), Second Drill (*rebattere* from the left), the Exchange of Thrusts, and Breaking the Thrust. This is short, easy to memorise and gets you started.

Then we have the Form itself, which has been developed over the last dozen years and was finalised in September 2014. This contains a reference to every part of *Il Fior di Battaglia* and an example of every major concept and technique, yet it can be done in about 45 seconds once you know it. It is therefore a set of chapter headings, under which you can store everything you ever learn about swordsmanship; and once you have filled out each chapter, you have a reference guide to your entire knowledge base.

I cannot state this too strongly: the Form is not the be-all and end-all; it's a beginning. When you write your own chapters, it becomes The Book of your Fiore knowledge and skill. Once that is established you can simply run through the Form at any time and identify the weakest link. Start working on that link, using the "attached" training material and the same set of skill development tools you learned in *The Medieval Longsword*, such as the Rule of Cs, Add a Step, Freeplay and so on. Then re-run the Form to see whether what you have been working on is still the weakest link. The Form is therefore a diagnostic tool, an aide-memoire, a mechanics exercise or a guide to the system; in fact, it is the core of your practice. This book is about filling in those chapters, both with more advanced training ideas and more difficult techniques, and it is also about providing some of the academic basis that makes this Art truly historical.

The major pitfall of this approach is that the organisation of the material in the Form has more to do with training space constraints and what felt good when designing it ("where do I want to go from here?") than it does with any overtly logical structure. It does not, for example, follow the order of these plays in any of the manuscripts. Nor is it arranged according to difficulty. So you may find yourself wanting to re-arrange things. That's fine: the structure is (as with all forms) at least partly arbitrary. You only need to have this canonically correct if you are following my school's syllabus and intending to grade within it. Otherwise, take this and make it your own!

When I was a kid, I spent some time casting little lead soldiers.

It was magic: you heat up the lead in a pan until it melts, pour it into the mould and wait for it to cool down, and out comes a cavalry officer, rifleman or whatever. We then had to trim off the inevitable little leaks and the rather large riser (the extra bit where you pour the metal in, called a "sprue" in the US). Then the figures were ready for painting. You can think of the Form in a similar way. The actions of the person doing the Form are moulded by the actions of the (imaginary or real) opponents, as well as by the overall training goals. As with the casting process, there are artefacts to be taken into account: little bits of metal that don't really belong, or some turns or steps that you wouldn't normally use but are necessary to keep the Form in the right shape. So long as you know what the Art should look like and what the applications are, or what a Royal Horse Guards trooper from 1815 is supposed to look like, the Form is useful. As soon as the mould (your understanding of which actions do what) gets sloppy, the Form becomes a shapeless, pointless mess.

So here is a rule to be followed whenever you think about any kind of Form: application first, Form second. We do this in class. When teaching the Form to students, we absolutely always do pair-drill (or handling drill) first, then the same actions solo, and then we add it to the Form. We never, ever, have students practising techniques that they don't know at least one application for, and we distinguish very clearly between a play or technique and a handling drill or skill-development exercise.

Veterans of my syllabus know full well that this is not the first version of the Form that we have had, which begs the question of "why the changes?" In short, training produces results: changes in the people who do the training. When my students progress I am, of course, looking for their idiosyncratic difficulties; but also, and more importantly in some ways, I am looking for the problems shared by their cohort. If everyone from a particular cohort is having the same problem, it must be the training that's at fault. At the beginning of 2014, the biggest cohort-wide issue was stopping when you shouldn't. Looking back over the basic syllabus that shaped these swordsmen, I saw that stopping was built into their training. In step one of every basic drill, the attacker does one strike and stops. The Form, as it was then, was full of single strikes followed by a pause or a reset to guard. No wonder everyone was stopping: it's what they trained to do! So I developed the *Farfalla di Ferro* (addressed in the next chapter) and changed step one of every basic drill to include at least a second strike, and then I rewrote the Syllabus Form (to howls of protest from some quarters). All of this revision was done with the help and co-operation of a cadre of senior students, over the internet and in person, drawing from almost every branch of the School. I signed off on the changes, but I didn't create them all myself.

Learning a Physical Art

Learning is a mental process – it happens only in the brain. There is no such thing as muscle memory, only ingrained neurological pathways that lead to actions being repeated. We suffer from the delusion that our physical actions are under the control of our conscious minds. This is not so. The wave of activity in the brain that triggers muscular movement actually occurs measurably *before* the wave of activity that signals the conscious decision to make that action. (This was demonstrated by Benjamin Libet in 1985 and confirmed by others since.) Of course, you can decide to extend your arm and then do so. But the brain gears itself up for making that arm movement before you consciously decide to do it. This has all sorts of interesting ramifications for free will, morality and so on; for our purposes (learning a physical art) it is enough to know, beyond reasonable doubt, that your conscious thought processes are not really needed for learning the actions of the Art. Indeed, more often than not, they get in the way. Try moving that same arm by explicitly, deliberately, contracting your deltoid, pectoral, tricep and latissimus dorsi muscles, plus all the rest of the arm muscles needed to keep the wrist straight, the elbow extending, and so on; all while adjusting your postural muscles to counteract the change in the distribution of your weight as your arm changes position, and so on and so forth. It can't be done. Instead we let a vastly sophisticated, incredibly fast-learning and wonderfully adaptive computer (i.e. our unconscious mind) do it all for us. All this wonder of nature needs is an example to follow (some kind of image will do) and some kind of feedback mechanism to let it know when it's performing the action better or worse than last time.

Given our consciousness-centric culture, it is outside of most students' experience to simply shut the conscious mind off and let the unconscious get to work. So it is a good idea to give that part of your mind something to do while you let the bigger, faster and cleverer part do the actual work. There is an old joke familiar to anyone who has been getting on with something useful while an idle layabout stands about getting in the way: "I love work: I can watch it all day". This quite accurately models the relationship between the two aspects of your mind. Let the worker work, and let the watcher sit idly by, watching.

It is critically important that the watcher does not get emotionally involved with what it is seeing. You may really, truly want to have a perfect *mandritto fendente* action, yet your current execution may be woefully below that standard. But any emotional response to that ("it's wrong!" Or: "it's crap!" Or: "I should be doing it better!") is always counter-productive. See it how it is, imagine it as you want it to be and leave the emotional judgments to things where they are actually important, such as guiding your moral actions or choosing a spouse.

Distraction works wonders when your mind is stuck in an unproductive rut. If you can just find something useful (or at least not counter-productive) for the mind to pay attention to, you can get out of the way of your own learning. The feeling of the ground under your feet is a good default choice.

Living with Perfectionism

One of the many reasons that teaching swordsmanship is the right career choice for me is that it is the one area of my life in which "good enough" is not even close to acceptable. "Excellent" is "okay for now, I suppose". This means that I am emotionally incapable of being satisfied with whatever level of technical and tactical skill I may attain. Back when I was a cabinet-maker (which I did professionally for five years), if it was good enough, I was happy with it. So I was perpetually frustrated, because I couldn't apply the necessary uncompromising will to excellence that marks a true craftsman. In swordsmanship, though, I simply cannot – will not – accept the current standard as "good enough". And I am therefore much more satisfied. This will seem a contradiction, but it isn't: *I am satisfied with progress made, not level attained.*

And it is that uncompromising, perpetual dissatisfaction with my current level that enables me to maintain the progress that I find so satisfying.

Perfection is unattainable in this lifetime. I have friends who make furniture, swords or other beautiful things, whose craftsmanship astonishes me. I will look at what they have made and gasp in awe and wonder at its shimmering perfection. They will then say something like: "well, it was a nightmare to do. That corner isn't quite right. And the proportions there are a bit off. It's crap, really. I'm not sure I should let it out of the workshop." But, and here's the irony: *they love their jobs.* It consumes and enlarges them.

I have seen many students suffer in training because of their desire to do everything perfectly. They let the fact that they cannot do it perfectly rob them of the pleasure from doing it more perfectly today than they could yesterday. My point here is that their suffering is unnecessary. Yes, your current level today is not as good as it might be tomorrow, but if this trend continues, it will be better tomorrow. So be happy!

So how to make the switch between focussing on the current level to focussing on progress made? There is no single, simple answer to this (is there ever?), but the following ideas have proved helpful to me.

1. Accept your fallible human nature. You will make mistakes, but ideally the mistakes you make today are smaller, less critical and just plain better than the mistakes you made yesterday. You have eternity to be perfect – once you're dead.
2. Record a video of yourself doing a basic exercise in training, and then don't look at it for a year. At that time record another video of you doing the same sort of training, and then compare the two clips. The improvement should be remarkable. If it isn't, your training methodology needs fixing.
3. Understand that as you improve, your ability to spot mistakes improves; so while you might have noticed huge mistakes in the beginning, thanks to your developing magnifying-glass vision, the much smaller mistakes you make

now are blown up and appear worse than they really are.

4. Just what is it about perfection that is so damn attractive? It seems to generally be taken to mean "so good that further progress is impossible". So, should you attain that state, the only thing to do is stop training because you're done. But swords are cool, so why would you want to stop training? Really, you can be perfect now: the sky is always perfect, but the sky is always changing. Be perfect like sky, not perfect like God.

Let me take my *mandritto fendente* as an example. By the objective standards of our community at present, it is pretty good; compared to the average beginner, it is excellent; and to me, it is profoundly flawed. Let's have a look at why.

Every blow has four phases: chamber, release, contact and withdrawal. (As an historical aside: George Silver identifies three such phases: bent = chambered; spent = contact; lying spent = the tempo after contact.)

When chambered, the blow is ready to go: the sword is withdrawn in some measure from the intended finishing point of the movement, such as lying in *posta di donna*. The question is, is that chamber perfect? In other words, is every molecule in my body in the perfect place such that releasing the blow requires no adjustment of any kind? No. But eliminating such adjustments eliminates telegraphing the blow to the opponent. This particular blow can start from many different positions: *fenestra, tutta porta di ferro* and *coda longa,* to name a few. It can also start as a continuation from another movement: after parrying from *zenghiaro,* for example, or after a feint in a different line. How smoothly does it flow from that movement? Not very. So, my chambering needs work. The stability drill might help.

Releasing the blow is pretty easy if the sword is already in motion, but quite hard if it is still. I have to overcome the inertia of the sword and make sure that the threat and opportunities presented to my opponent truly are *exactly* as I think they are. If I think I have presented no opportunity to counterattack and I'm right, either the blow lands or the blow is parried; or if the opponent does counterattack, his action will fail and I will strike. If I am wrong, the counterattack might kill me. Also, the moment of release is the most difficult part of the blow to get right, because any imperfection in the chamber will lead my body to do a semi-conscious mini-chambering action, which will tell my opponent that I'm on my way. If I can control this, I can feed him that tell and profit from his reaction to it, or I can hide it and strike without telegraphing. I can also adjust the rate of acceleration from "go like hell" all-out maximum speed (get there before the parry arrives); or to start slow and finish fast (trick him into a too-slow parry); to start fast and slow down a little, then speed up again (watch that fast parry go by, then hit him) – all within the time taken to get from *donna* to *longa*. Is my release perfect? Not even close. So I'd better get in front of a mirror or video camera and watch it. The blow should be perfectly supported on contact. This means that all the energy in the blow goes into the target, and the equal and opposite reaction that Newtonian physics demand is routed perfectly through my sword, through my grip, down my body and into the ground. Or rather, if I choose it to be so, it is. When hitting students or colleagues in free fencing, it is better to break that connection to minimise damage. But breaking that connection must be done right, or the force of the blow may be absorbed in my wrist, neck, shoulder, hip or knee (to name the usual problem spots), and it can cause damage over time. If the blow is supposed to be unsupported (such as in a *zwerchau*), then controlling the impact is even more challenging because there is no structure behind the edge with which to manipulate the impact. It's a good thing we are looking at a nice, simple and supported *mandritto fendente*, then. Is my contact perfect? Um, no. Striking the tyre, stroking the pell, static pressure grounding exercises and free fencing may all help.

After contact I must withdraw safely: there is no sense in just leaving the sword stuck in the target. So, is this blow intended to strike through (to *zenghiaro*, for example) or to stay in *posta longa*? If through, depending on what I am hitting, it might be best to support the blow all the way through (e.g. when cutting targets like tatami) or to break on contact (e.g. when hitting friends). If cutting through, does that action perfectly chamber the next blow, or perfectly create the guard in which I wish to finish? Cutting through also requires the tactical circumstances in which to withdraw. It might be safer to change the blow and leave the sword in the centre, especially if the blow failed for some reason (such as not being perfect). Can I always, reliably and at full speed adjust my withdrawal accordingly? No. I'd better work on that then. Tyre, pell, free fencing, drills with degrees of freedom and form may all help.

So, we have now established the profound imperfections of my *mandritto fendente*. But I can fence with the best in my community and hit them with it, so it's not useless. It also rarely fails to slice through tatami, so it's not useless. It also hits the tyre pretty hard, so, you guessed it, it's not useless. I am much better at manipulating my opponent's expectations of the blow now than I was five years ago. So that's getting better. I don't think I've improved on power much in that time, so perhaps I should work more on that. My chambering has improved noticeably since I regularly incorporated the stability drill into my training, so that's a double win: I developed a useful drill and improved a blow.

Okay, that's the mechanics (structure and flow) of the blow addressed. What about tactics (time and measure)? *When* is this the right blow to use? It is rarely wrong to strike a good *mandritto fendente*: I picked a good general purpose blow for that very reason. But can I use this as a parry? A feint? A counterattack? In which measures is it best? If you have ever seen someone trying to land a *mandritto fendente* when they have the opponent's arms enveloped in their own left arm, it's a pitiful sight. Pommel strike, hilt strike or pull the sword back and thrust would all work better. Though the *fendente* is clearly implied in the text and picture of the ninth play of the *zogho stretto*, which shows the player wrapped up in a *ligadura mezana*. So, wait, perhaps there is work to be done here ... pair drills; the plays from the treatise in which they appear, in their canonical forms and in variations; and free fencing may all help.

Perfectionism, the emotional incapability of accepting less than perfection, is the engine that drives excellence in all its forms. It also cripples many swordsmanship careers before they even start. It is a powerful and overwhelming force, so treat it carefully and harness it to your goals.

This book covers the next level in your Fiore longsword training. It contains two complete Forms – a short one, known as the Cutting Drill, and a longer one, known as the Syllabus Form – as well as a sword handling drill called the *Farfalla di Ferro* (the "Iron

Butterfly"). These are all core training tools we use at The School of European Swordsmanship. These Forms have developed over the course of the last decade; as my interpretation of Fiore's Art changed, and the needs of the students became more sophisticated, so the Forms changed right alongside. A Form is a tool, a means to an end. The purpose of it is to store a huge amount of information about Fiore's system in a finite space; the steps of the Form act as loci for memory, to ingrain correct mechanics, and to provide an overview of the key elements of the system. I think of each step of the Form as the heading for a chapter in a book; once you know the Form you have the table of contents. Your job, then, is to fill out each chapter according to your needs and interests. This book represents one way of doing that. Before we go into detail, let's establish some training principles.

Run a Diagnostic

Training progresses in periods of apparent stagnation punctuated by irregular leaps, and it is natural for you to feel like you have hit a plateau at certain stages. The key to getting past the plateau is having a system for discovering the weakest link in your skills, and then strengthening it specifically. The process goes like this:

- run a diagnostic,
- find the weakest link,
- strengthen the weakest link through specific practise, and
- run the diagnostic again.

When you run the diagnostic for the second time, there are three possible outcomes.

1. Nothing has changed. The same thing is the weakest link. So clearly your specific practise needs to change. Find another way to fix it.
2. The same thing is the weakest link, but it's better than it was. In this case, keep doing the same specific practise, and then test again.
3. Something else is the weakest link. Choose a specific practise to fix it, and then run the process again.

Every time you show up for class or practise in your group or on your own, you ought to be working on a specific thing. This could be a matter of breadth (adding new knowledge to your base), or it could be a matter of depth (taking something you know and making it work better).

One of the best tools in the martial artist's toolbox for diagnosing problems and adding depth or breadth is Form. Form is the primary means of storing the Art and disseminating it in many traditional martial arts. This is less common in Europe, but we do still find Forms, especially in the sixteenth-century Italian sources. Simply put, a Form is a set of motions that you repeat, either solo or with a partner. Every set drill is a kind of Form.

I think that training ought to be focussed and goal-oriented. The goal in any fencing context is to strike without being struck, so any problem can be thought of as "I'm getting hit" or "I'm not hitting". Drills are the means by which we fix either of these core problems.

Let's start with the "I'm getting hit" problem. Here is a snazzy little flowchart:

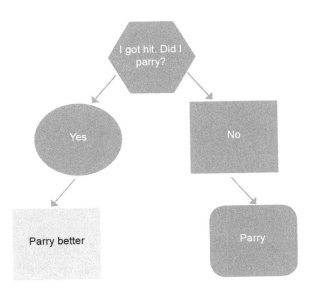

The Fencer's Flowchart

Yes, it boils down to this: the only reason you ever get hit is because you failed to parry. The hit is never wrong. This is really important. When we are past the point of teaching beginners the absolute basics, we don't solve the problem of being hit by changing the attack. The attack is supposed to hit. So whatever your current fencing problem is, here are the steps to fix it.

1. Reproduce the problem. If you can't reproduce it, it was either a fluke, and so not something that can be trained against, or you didn't understand what happened. You can't fix training problems that you don't understand so, if that happens, find somebody to explain what happened to you. Your opponent or your teacher might do that.
2. Analyse why you are getting hit. You are either doing the right thing but not well enough, or you are doing the wrong thing. So the problem is either technical or tactical. These have quite different solutions.

Technical problems are solved by training the technique in increasingly challenging contexts. In short, slow down until it works, and then ramp up the speed and power gradually until you can do it at the necessary level. I think of this as solving problems of incompetence.

Tactical problems are solved by choosing a better solution at the critical moment, which you learn to do by using drills with ever increasing degrees of freedom. I think of this as solving problems of ignorance.

Whatever drill you are doing should be solving a specific problem of either ignorance or incompetence, making you wiser and better. (The specific details of how to use pressure and degrees of freedom are in *The Swordsman's Quick Guide* part 3, *Preparing for Freeplay*. They are also described in *The Medieval Longsword*.)

I have put all this together in another nifty flowchart. The original was done by me in Scapple, which is a great app with which to think, but it doesn't do pretty charts. Several kind and lovely readers have sent me much prettier versions. This one, by Andrew R. Mizener, is the clearest.

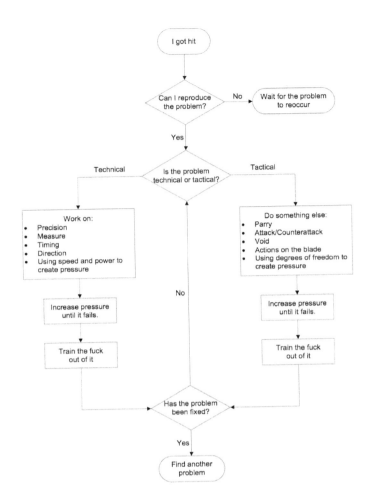

How to Create a Form

It helps to know how forms are created in order to use them efficiently. Any form has, at least, the following elements.

- Techniques: the heart of the Art itself.
- Attribute training exercises: technical studies intended to generate specific skills or strengths, such as jumps for leg strength, handling drills for weapons, and all sorts of things that you wouldn't use in a fight but which make you a better martial artist.
- Connecting steps: steps included to make the pattern of the Form coherent and repeatable, or to make it fit into the available training space.

We are so accustomed to using forms in our training that whenever my senior students are presented with a lot of new material, or a new system, they will tend to write a form to preserve it. A recent example of this was at the Fiore Extravaganza seminar in July 2015, in which we covered a lot of pollax material. The students asked if we could spend some of the seminar time creating a form to store the things they had learned, so we went over Fiore's pollax plays and some stuff from *Jeu de la Hache*, and I used the next few sessions to teach them how to create a form in a systematic, rational and useful way.

We started by deciding what the form was for, and then what the technical content ought to be.

The following text is what we came up with.

What is it For?
- Self-Improvement. This was the first thing mentioned. It is a little vague but a good base from which to work.
- Memory Guide. The form should make it easier for students to recall aspects of the pollax material.
- Flow/Mechanics. Practising the form should ingrain the correct movement style and habits, enabling fluent and powerful actions.
- Expandable. The form should be built in a way that allows the various actions to be expanded upon, to trigger memory cascades and to create loci for memorising other material.

This led us to consider the next question:

What Should it Contain?
The first thing that was mentioned was the guards of the axe, so that became our starting point. Around that came grip and handling drills, ways of exploiting armour, strikes, disarms, locks, takedowns and parries. This became our list of things to cover.

Many forms come in two parts. The Syllabus Form and the Cutting Drill are obvious examples, both covered in this book, but I have come across the same thing in many other martial arts.

We decided to start with applications, which of course must be trained in pairs. Then it struck me that, once we had a curriculum of pair drills, we could make part one the defensive actions (remedies) and part two the offensive actions (attacks and counter-remedies). This would allow us to embed the stimuli for the various actions of the form within the form itself.

So we started with a pair drill, the defence of *dente di zenghiaro* against *posta di donna*, and added *posta di donna*'s counter-remedy. These became step one of parts one and two respectively.

Over the course of a couple of hours, we came up with three solid drills beginning with the following pairs of guards: *donna* versus *zenghiaro*, *posta breve la serpentina* versus *vera croce*, and *coda longa* versus *posta di finestra la sinestra*. I checked the various aspects of technique against the list of things to cover as we covered them, and continued to do so until we had covered everything.

We then considered tactics. By this stage in the development, we had included attacks, feints, yielding to parries ("go around"), parry-riposte and invitations.

But we were not completely satisfied: counterattacks were not well represented, and neither were crossings of the axe. So we chose to add a fourth drill, with *vera croce* opposed by *fenestra la sinestra*, which would include the things we found lacking.

Now we had to put these pieces in order and glue them together with axe handling drills and references to *Jeu de la Hache* (which is the best medieval source for this weapon, I think). The first question was how to tie the two halves together. It was tricky, so we shelved it and worked on the easier ones.

Ordering the drills was easy enough. We put them in the same order as the pairs of guards shown in the Getty manuscript (MS). I wrote down the starting guard and finishing guard for each drill, which went as follows.

Part 1:
- *Vera croce*, finishes in a one-handed *fenestra destra*.
- *Dente di zenghiaro*, finishes in guard of the cross (from *Jeu*).
- *Fenestra sinestra*, finishes with your axe in one hand between the opponent's legs, left foot forwards.

Part 2:

- *Breve la serpentina*, finishes with a takedown, right foot forwards.
- *Donna destra*, finishes in guard of the cross.
- *Coda longa*, finishes in a *ligadura sottana* with the left hand.
- *Fenestra sinestra*, finishes in *posta breve la serpentina*. From here you need to be able to go to the end position (whatever that will be), back to the beginning of the form or to the beginning of part two.

So we then worked together to make useful and interesting "magic glue" to tie the parts together. We were careful to practise these together, to make sure that the form could be done in class and in our salle, and we added several turns to reduce the form's footprint.

The last task was to create the segue between parts one and two. We started out by calling it the "Butterfly", but I thought that was un-axe-like and so we called it the "Dragon" instead. This was apposite, because one thing the students wanted to include was some of the queue/pedale/tail of the axe material from *Jeu de la Hache* and, as readers of *Veni Vadi Vici* know, the dragon strikes by lashing with its tail. The Dragon had to be very clearly not a pair drill, though, or we would end up creating another application set, leaving us with a form that would get longer and longer. In the end I came up with an exercise based on my own arm-conditioning drills with a long stick.

Once the form was complete, we summarised the process we had used to create it. Here's the summary.

The Process:

1. Purpose: decide what the form is for.
2. Components: decide what applications and other elements it should include, such as tactics, guards and so on.
3. Survey: check the components to make sure you have all the necessary aspects covered, and finalise the total content.
4. Organise: order the components.
5. Combine: create the magic glue that ties the components together, taking into account physical space constraints.

6. Test and bug fix: this requires a feedback mechanism and is much easier with a group or team.
7. Practise: train it!

This raises the questions of how to train the Form and what the potential risks of form training are. The primary risk of form training can be summarised as "it becomes ballet". Compliant opponents allow your technique to become sloppy: form replaces function. There is also the risk of over-specialisation, in that you can confuse the content of the Form with the entire content of the Art. Drilling the applications properly should prevent balletisation, and expanding every step should prevent over-specialisation. But this is not an easy process, which is one of the reasons for writing this book.

In brief, the form can be used for solo practice and with partners to train applications; each step can be expanded to include other elements; it is a memory palace in which to store the things you have learned; and it can be used as a diagnostic.

All of this took place in a single morning. The longsword Syllabus Form that this book describes took about a decade of tinkering.

The Cutting Drill is the first proper form that most of my students learn. As with other forms, it comes in two parts: the first is very basic, and the second is more complex. It includes just about everything you need to know to fight with the sword; every strike and every kind of technique is actually represented, if you know how to read it.

Part one has full blows and half blows, and cuts and thrusts, all from right and left, and from high and low. It also has *posta di donna* on right and left, *tutta porta di ferro*, *posta di dente di zenghiaro*, and *posta longa*; so it has guards high and low, left and right, and in the middle.

Part two has the breaking of the thrust, the *punta falsa*, a pommel strike, parrying from the left, and using *bicorno*; it also includes *fenestra* on the right and *donna* on the left (rear-weighted), as well as *porta di ferro la mezana* and both *mezani* blows. I'll take you through the whole thing step by step, of course, but at this stage I want you to get some idea of how forms can be used as .zip files to store simply huge amounts of information about a martial system.

Way back in 2001, shortly after I opened the first branch of The School of European Swordsmanship, I wrote a form for the students to practise. Looking back, it was so bad, so inefficient and so riven with errors of interpretation, and with incorrect actions and applications, that I blush to even mention it. But, and this is a *big* but, at that time it was state-of-the-art. We used it regularly, and by June 2001 it was already finished enough that I taught a class on it in the International Swordplay and Martial Arts Convention in Lansing, Michigan. That Form stood us in good stead for a couple of years, and it didn't really change in that time. But by 2006 it was clearly so out of date that we had stopped using it altogether and, with some of the senior students, I set to work on writing this one. We got the basic idea down quite quickly: start with drawing the sword, include references to the most common plays and get some sword handling in. The form was stable by the end of 2007, and it was trained diligently by a generation of students. But as our Art developed, we (the senior students, branch leaders, class leaders and I) started to find that it was inculcating some undesirable habits, not least the tendency to do one thing and then stop. It also did not properly incorporate my ground-breaking interpretive breakthrough regarding blade relationship and the *zogho largo/zogho stretto* distinction.

We started work on rewriting the form in 2013, and it became canon (i.e. it was formally incorporated in its new guise into the syllabus) in 2014. This led one of my students to produce a "Hitler discovers ..." video, which you might enjoy: https://youtu.be/licd-PAilZTE

The main changes were an increased focus on flow (the older version was rather stop-start-stop-start) and an expansion to include more of the *largo/stretto* distinctions.

I'm sure that if we put a work party together to write a new form from scratch, we would come up with something quite different. Yet the purpose of this book is not to present the last word in longsword training and form writing, but to give you a broader, deeper understanding of Fiore's Art as I interpret it; it's also to give you a broader, deeper insight into how to create and use forms for your own purposes.

One more thing

You may notice that sometimes I use the masculine pronoun, and sometimes the feminine, to describe the actions of the opponents in this form. The one doing the form is "you". I have done this before, and it caused quite a stir for no good reason I can think of. I am a man: I think of myself as "he". So when I am describing my actions to you, but in the third person, I'll say "he attacks", "he is annoying", and so on. When I am describing what someone else is doing, I almost always have a specific student in mind; my students are (or identify as) male (about 65%), female, (about 34%) and other/in between/not sure yet/prefer not to say (about 1%). Whichever pronoun I use when descibing an action will depend upon which student I am thinking of at the time. Ville attacks? Break his arm. Satu attacks? Break her arm. Please don't read any more into it than that.

PART ONE

THE CUTTING DRILL

Let us begin with a revision of part one of the Cutting Drill, which you already know from *The Medieval Longsword.*

1. Begin in *posta di donna destra.*
2. Cut *mandritto fendente* through *longa* to *dente di zenghiaro,* passing.
3. Cut *roverso sottano* to *longa,* false edge, passing.
4. Go to *donna destra.*
5. Cut *mandritto fendente* to *longa.*
6. Go to *donna la sinistra.*
7. Cut *roverso fendente* to *tutta porta di ferro.*
8. Cut *mandritto sottano* to *longa,* false edge, passing.
9. Go to *donna la sinistra.*
10. Cut *roverso fendente* to *longa,* passing.

At this stage, return the sword to *posta di donna* and start again.

Common Problems

The most common errors when striking are as follows.

- Wrong start position: if you have to adjust anything before the blow starts, the position must be wrong.
- Inefficient path: any deviation from a straight line causes unnecessary delay, slowing the blow down.
- Excessive tension: the body should be as relaxed as possible before, during and after the blow. The sword is already hard, so you don't need to be.
- Initiation: every movement feels like it starts in the point of the sword, as if it is being dragged to the target with your body following on behind. Stepping before you strike

gives an impression of power (it does make it easier to hit hard), but will result in your presenting a target (your face) before making your opponent deal with a threat (your sword).

The primary tools for self-correction of these errors are the stability drill, slow blows and the use of a video camera or mirror to establish any difference between what you are doing and what you think you are doing.

There are four actions you need to know before you can make sense of part two, three of which you should remember from *The Medieval Longsword*: breaking the thrust from *fenestra* on the right (pp. 108-111); the parry of the sword in one hand (pp. 147-152); and thrusting with *bicorno* (pp. 121-123). Make sure they are fresh in your mind before going to the next step, which is the missing link for this drill: the *punta falsa*.

The Punta Falsa

There is rarely only one solution to a given problem. The pommel strike is fine against a defender parrying from the right, but there is a better option. One of the most stylish techniques in the system is the *punta falsa*, which translates literally as "false thrust". Fiore's instructions are very detailed:

> "*I show that I am coming with great force to strike the player with a middle blow in the head [in other words, make sure he sees it coming]. And immediately that he makes the cover I strike his sword lightly. And immediately turn my sword to the other side, grabbing my sword with my left hand about at the middle. And I place the thrust immediately in the throat or in the chest...*" (Translation mine.)

This is the eighteenth play of the second Master of the *zogho largo*, and so in its basic form it is done as a riposte after a successful parry of the first attack (as shown by said master). It can, of course, be done any time there is an opening to throw the *mezano* feint, but let's start out being strictly canonical. We bring this to life like so:

1. attacker strikes *mandritto fendente*;
2. parry from the right into *frontale*, beating the attacker's sword wide;
3. keep the motion going to strike a *mandritto mezano*, leaving your hands high and to the left;
4. attacker parries with *frontale*;
5. strike lightly on his sword and turn your sword hand over, turning your sword around the midpoint;
6. reach for the middle of your sword with your left hand; and
7. thrust him in the mask, with an *accrescere* if needed.

Janne parries Satu's blow, and shows her the strong mezano, which Satu parries; so Janne turns his sword and grabs his blade by the middle, placing his thrust and parrying her riposte.

Common Problems with the Punta Falsa

Several things can go wrong when you're practising the *punta falsa*. The most common errors are as follows.

- Starting too close. Make sure you leave enough space to turn your sword when attacking.
- Making the turn too big, and ending up with a cut or slap instead of a thrust. Let the point lead you in.
- Failing to get the sword from one side to the other. This last is not a problem: in the Bolognese style, staying on the same side with this action is actually called the *punta falsa*. If it happens, make sure your entry is fast and deep enough that the defender's strike will fail and, if you can, redirect your left hand to control his sword arm instead of your blade.
- Cross-handed pairs will find that the *punta falsa only* works when there is a forehand (*mandritto*) *mezano* being met by

a parry on the inside of the attack. This allows the turn to half-sword, which is only mechanically possible from this situation. A left-hander will therefore need to strike the *mezano* to generate a parry from the opponent's left side; right-handers need to draw a parry from the opponent's right side.

Countering the Punta Falsa

The counter is given as the last play of *zogho largo*; the instruction is simplicity itself, but the action is very counterintuitive for most people. The exact nature of the blade action and the relationship between the weapons was first figured out by Sean Hayes, at The Western Martial Arts Workshop (WMAW), in 2006. We had just attended a lecture on the manuscript and seen really high resolution scans for the first time – the scans were so clear that we could see places where the manuscript had been corrected (by scraping off the original ink and redrawing a line). The counter-remedy master's sword was suddenly, clearly, on the inside of the player's sword (i.e. the one trying to do the *punta falsa*). I will never forget the time, half an hour later, when Sean tried out this interpretation on me and sold it in one go as my attack collapsed and his point magically appeared in my mask …

To make it work, then:

1. attack with a *mandritto fendente;*
2. defender parries from the right into *frontale*, beating your sword wide; defender keeps the motion going to strike a *mandritto mezano*, leaving his hands high and to the left;
3. you parry his *mezano* with *frontale;*
4. defender strikes lightly on your sword and, as he turns his sword hand over, you turn yours, inside the defender's movement, passing diagonally left with your left foot;
5. you reach for the middle of your sword with your left hand; and
6. you strike, bringing your right foot back and around.

Inside (ideal) and outside (okay).
As Janne turns his sword, Satu turns hers, staying inside Janne's turn,
stepping offline to her left and thrusting Janne in the face.

Perhaps the most common problem when attempting this counter is ending up outside your opponent's sword. Don't worry, that's how everybody did this play for years. It works, it just takes longer. It can also be documented in other sources, so it's even historically accurate. But if your partner does it, yield immediately to then pommel strike on the other side.

As Satu turns her sword, ending outside Janne's, Janne parries it with his blade on her left wrist and strikes her in the face with his pommel.

You can see this play in all the versions of *Il Fior di Battaglia*. Here it is in the Getty MS:

Now that the components of the drill are all present, let's string them together as a solo drill (or form).

1. Begin in *fenestra destra*. Break the thrust with the *acrescere fora di strada, passo ala traversa*, driving the opponent's sword down; then cut his throat with a *roverso mezano* and, as he falls backwards in a shower of gore, finish the job with a *roverso fendente*, passing forwards into *tutta porta di ferro*.

2. From *tutta porta di ferro*, parry through *frontale*, show him the strong *mezano*, turn the sword to the *punta falsa* and *acrescere* forwards to thrust. If he parries that, smash your pommel down onto his face while passing forwards with your right foot. *Volta stabile* to the guard of the Master of the sword in one hand.

3. From the guard of the Master of the sword in one hand, your opponent attacks with a *mandritto fendente*. Beat it up and away while doing an *acrescere*, and strike, cleaving him in twain as your sword swings through to *donna la sinestra*, the momentum carrying you into a *volta stabile*, so you end up rear-weighted.

4. From *donna la sinestra*, slam your point into his face while passing forwards using *bicorno*, to make his exchange impossible and his parry very difficult.

And there you have it. Part two. Do you notice how, all of a sudden, I'm not talking about safety or co-operation. You are doing bloody murder – and enjoying it, with no moral consequences, *because your opponent is imaginary*. This is one of the great things about solo training. You can apply every technique with full intent and power, to the proper targets, and not go to jail.

But: solo training can allow sloppiness to creep in, because there are no external checks on your judgement of timing and measure. So now you should also do this as a pair drill.

Note that you have done every one of these actions as pair drills, many times, before. So we string them together, something like this list.

1. Your partner is in *donna la sinestra*; you are in *fenestra destra* (and do I really have to remind you to put your masks on? If so, please put this book down and go back to *The Medieval Longsword* for a while).

2. He attacks with a thrust, using *bicorno*.

3. You break it to the ground, cut his throat and hit him in the head as he passes backwards.

4. You end up in *tutta porta di ferro*; he resets and attacks with a *mandritto fendente*.

5. You parry, beating it wide, and sucker him with a *punta falsa*. Whether he parries it or not, continue to the pommel strike, and await his next attack in the guard of the Master of the sword in one hand.

6. When he attacks, beat his sword wide and cut, using the proper footwork, and end up in *donna la sinestra*. Your partner goes to *fenestra destra* and, as you attack with your devastating thrust, he breaks it …

So the drill is circular, and you will start to get sloppy as it builds up momentum. That's okay. Go back to doing it perfectly on your own, then back to the circular drill, and so on.

Now that the cutting drill is complete, you can see how it is structured.

Part one is a basic curriculum of the most common strikes, which naturally encodes the four basic drills: first drill, second drill, break and exchange.

Part two plays variations on them: a break from *fenestra*; the *punta falsa* that starts out like first drill; the parry from the left, like second drill, but from the guard of the Master of the sword in one hand; and a thrust in *bicorno* from the left, which prevents the possibility of an exchange.

This is a good start, and it should give you an idea of what's to come when we look at the Form.

FARFALLA DI FERRO

The *Farfalla di Ferro* (the "Iron Butterfly") is a sword handling drill intended to give you a smooth command of the weapon. I recommend working on the up-down-around-around drill and the Six Grips handling drill first. You can find these drills on the wiki. The Farfalla di Ferro is all about effortless, continuous motion. We divide it into two parts for easy assimilation (as we do with the Cutting Drill and the Syllabus Form).

I thought about using photos to illustrate this, but it would have doubled the length of the book. Instead, there is a video online that you should watch several times before trying to work out the drill. It is here: http://www.swordschool.com/wiki/index.php/ Farfalle_di_Ferro

Part One

1. Start in *posta di donna destra* and strike *mandritto fendente* with a pass.
2. Let the *mandritto fendente* follow through past *dente di zenghiaro* and up to *fenestra la sinestra* (no step).
3. Strike a *roverso fendente* with a pass while turning the sword round the middle of the blade, through *tutta porta di ferro*, past *coda longa*, and up to *fenestra destra*.
4. Turn the sword, from *fenestra destra*, around the middle of the blade to strike a *mandritto fendente*.
5. Continue from step one.

Part Two

We normally teach part two in stages: first going forwards, then backwards and then adding it to part one. The key motion is two *sottani* blows on each side: false-edge true-edge, false-edge true-edge, and with a pass on each true-edge *sottano*.

1. Go to *tutta porta di ferro* and strike a *mandritto sottano* with the false edge to *posta longa*, standing still.
2. Continue the motion in a *molinello* into a true edge *mandritto sottano*, passing forwards.
3. Continue the motion into a false edge *roverso sottano*, standing still.
4. *Molinello* into a true edge *roverso sottano*, passing forwards to *fenestra destra*.
5. Allow the sword to continue its motion into a false edge *mandritto sottano* to *longa*, and then continue as before.

When this is comfortable, replace each pass forwards with a pass backwards. Make sure that the path behind you is clear beforehand, of course.

Then we add it to part one. As we arrive in *fenestra destra*, at the end of part one, the sword is rising and going forwards.

1. Keep that motion going and do a *meza volta/tutta volta* combination, passing forwards with your right foot and pivoting round with your left to face the opposite direction, leading the point of the sword into a false edge *mandritto sottano*.
2. Keeping the motion going, do the true edge *mandritto sottano* (you won't need to step because you are already right foot forwards); flow through to the false edge *roverso sottano*, passing backwards (*tornare*) and allowing the motion to continue into a true edge *roverso sottano*.
3. As the sword is rising, turn your body 180° clockwise and allow the sword to fall into a *roverso fendente*, passing forwards with your right foot. Continue the process; you are now back in part one, beginning on the left side.
4. The sword is rising into *fenestra la sinestra*: allow the thrust to segue into a *meza volta/tutta volta* combination while passing with the left foot and bringing the right behind, and follow with the natural false edge *roverso sottano*. Continue the pattern until you find yourself back at the beginning.

Does this sound like a lot of stuff to remember? Well, it is. If you have difficulty stringing these actions together, go back and do the component parts: parts one and two, and also the footwork turns, until the instructions make sense.

This is not supposed to be easy; it's a handling drill, to be practised until fluent. When it is fluent, and not a moment before, go to the next level, which is making the turns of the sword smaller.

In its basic form, the *Farfalla di Ferro* is big: the sword arm is turning around the shoulder joint for most of the actions. Even when the *fendenti* are done with a turn around the *meza spada*, the sword falls through the low guards and then up back to *fenestra*. It's swoopy, lovely and, once the flow is there, very easy.

So now do every turn around the middle of the sword – even the four *sottani*. This forces you to make tight and precise motions, just as you would when crossed at the middle of the swords with an opponent.

Then come the applications. Obviously, every one of the blows – except the thrusts from *fenestra* – are both parries and strikes. They can also be winds, binds, feints and counterattacks. They can be done going forwards, backwards or to either side. Go through every blow in the drill (*mandritto fendente*, thrust from the left; *roverso fendente*, thrust from the right; *mandritto sottano*, with either edge; and *roverso sottano*, with either edge), and see how many applications you can come up with for each of them. There is also a video online here: http://www.swordschool.com/wiki/index.php/Farfalle_di_Ferro It's called "Applications to the Farfalla di Ferro", and watching it will help you out if you get stuck.

You will need at least part one of the *Farfalla di Ferro* before attempting the Syllabus Form.

PART TWO

THE SYLLABUS FORM

The Syllabus Form is a set of applications, handling drills and other actions, all combined in order to make a useful and convenient training tool. As I wrote in the introduction, all forms are made up of the following three components.

1. Techniques: the heart of the Art itself.
2. Attribute training exercises: technical studies intended to generate specific skills or strengths, such as jumps for leg strength, handling drills for weapons, and all sorts of things that you wouldn't use in a fight but which make you a better martial artist.
3. Connecting steps: steps included to make the pattern of the Form coherent and repeatable, or to make it fit into the available training space.

Perhaps the single most important thing to start with is this: *you must know which is which.* Mistaking a leg-strength drill for a combat-ready application can be fatal!

So let's have a look at the whole thing. It has seventeen "steps", which are made up of a total of about 50 movements. Each step is a play from the treatise or a handling drill of some description. I will then break each step out into its own chapter and go through it in depth and detail.

To keep you oriented, the direction you are facing is specified at every step. The direction you are originally facing in is designated as north, and the direction you are facing at the end of each step is noted with a single, double or triple capital letter. So, N, S, E, W, NE, SSW, and so on. Whatever direction you are facing at the beginning of Step I is N.

All left-right instructions are for right-handers; left-handers should reverse them. More confusingly, north and south remain the same for left-handers as for right-handers, but east and west are reversed for lefties. Also, guards with left or right in their names (such as *posta di donna destra*) should be reversed. I have worked those differences through for you here, but I will not double the length of the book by doing so in every chapter. In any case, once the Form is clear in your natural orientation, you should learn it again with the other hand. It's good for your brain!

The Form, Right-Handed

Step I: Drawing the sword.

This is a defence against a dagger attack, as shown on f21v. I will include the images from the treatise when we unpack each step later in the book. All references are to the Getty MS unless stated otherwise.

Holding the sword and scabbard against the shoulder, step back offline to your right with your right foot and parry the dagger strike by cutting down from above against the crook of the attacker's elbow. Keeping pressure on the elbow, draw your sword, thrust low and then thrust high in *fenestra destra*. N.

Step II: Sword handling one, from the *Farfalla di Ferro*.

Cut a *mandritto fendente* with a pass through to *dente di zenghiaro*; continue the motion up to *fenestra sinestra* and thrust with a *roverso punta*. Then turn a *roverso fendente* with a pass through *posta di coda longa* and a *volta stabile* to *posta di fenestra*, ending in a rear-weighted stance. N.

Step III: Exchange of thrust.

This is a defence against a thrust to the face. Both attack and defence are from *fenestra destra*; this is an application of the ninth and tenth plays of the Master of the *zogho largo* crossed at the middle of the swords, f28v.

Exchange of thrust with an *accrescere fora di strada* and *passo ala traversa*; continue to the hilt grab and disarm (with *meza volta* (left foot) and *tutta volta*), and then thrust low. E.

Step IV: Feint.

This is partly a handling drill. It's the sort of action that is too complex to be likely to work well in combat, but if you can do it at speed or in freeplay then you must have learned some critical skills of timing, tactics and sword handling.

Feint a low thrust with one hand and, as your opponent exchanges, disengage underneath, wind to high one-handed thrust and pass diagonally forward with your right foot. As your opponent parries, yield and cut a *mandritto fendente*, sidestepping with your left foot, ending in *donna la sinestra*. Look over right shoulder. S.

Step V: *Rompere di punta,* backhand.

This is done against a thrust to the face from *fenestra destra* (creating the same setup with roles reversed that we saw in step one of part two of the cutting drill. It is not shown in the Getty MS, but you can see it on carta 21A of the *Pisani Dossi*).

Break the thrust with a *roverso fendente*, with an *accrescere fora di strada* and *passo ala traversa*. End in *tutta porta di ferro*. SSW.

Note, when doing this in a pair drill, you should cut the throat with a *mandritto mezano*. This is elided in the Form with the next step.

Step VI: *Rompere di punta,* forehand.

This is done against a thrust to the belly from *dente di zenghiaro*, and in the normal way.

Breaking the thrust: grab the blade with a *mandritto fendente*, keeping the hands low, and *accrescere fora di strada* and *passo ala traversa*; then cut his throat with a false edge *roverso mezano* to the throat. Follow through with a *roverso fendente* to his head, passing to *tutta porta di ferro*. S.

Step VII: *Rebattere,* forehand.

This is done against a *mandritto fendente* to the head, like in First Drill but with a couple of tweaks and with alternative footwork.

Parry with *frontale* and cut over his arms with a *mandritto fendente*, with a *passo fora di strada*, and then thrust to chest in *bicorno* with a pass forwards. SE.

Note the *frontale-longa-bicorno* sequence in the hands. Note also the alternative footwork to how we do it in First Drill, and indeed to how Fiore describes the footwork on f27v, where it is the first and second plays of the Master of the *zogho largo* crossed at the middle of the swords.

Step VIII: Master of the sword in one hand.

This is done against a *mandritto fendente* to the head. As you parry, the attacker binds or resists the parry so you cannot beat his sword away and strike, and instead must enter. See f22v.

Lower your sword to the guard of the Master of the sword in one hand, let go with your left hand and look over your shoulder. (NW.)

Rebattere with a true edge *roverso sottano* accompanied by an *acrescimento*, while extending the left hand forward. The attacker resists the parry, so you pass in with a *ligadura mezana* and thrust him in the throat.

Continue with a *mandritto fendente* with a pass (right foot) and *tutta volta*, 135° round, finishing in *dente di zenghiaro*. S.

Step IX: *Rebattere,* backhand.

This is done against a *mandritto fendente* to the head, exactly as in Second Drill. See f33r.

Parry with false edge *roverso sottano* accompanied by an *acressere fora di strada*, and immediately execute a *mandritto fendente*, which goes through *longa* and through *dente di zenghiaro* and (with a *volta stabile*) to rear-weighted *posta di donna sinestra*. S.

Step X: Sword handling two.

This is the longest blow in the Art, and the idea is to do it hard and fast and yet be able to instantaneously reverse its direction into a thrust. Good luck.

Roverso fendente with pass to *coda longa*, and immediately thrust to *bicorno* with another pass. S.

Step XI: *Punta falsa.*

This is done against a *mandritto fendente* to the head from the NE. See f29v. Note the alternative footwork, which comes from the defence of the dagger against a sword thrust on f21r.

Parry with *frontale*, with a *tornare* of the left foot, so your opponent's sword is beaten wide. Show him your strong *mezano* to the face with a diagonal sidestep of the right foot (*passo fora di strada*) and, as your opponent parries, execute the *punta falsa* with a pass in with the left foot. NE.

As your opponent parries, throw the hilt of your sword at his head with your right hand shifting to the blade, as in the *Master of Sword-As-Axe*, f24v.

Volta stabile and shift the right foot to face north. Switch your right hand back to the grip so you are now in *vera croce*. N.

Step XII: First play of the sword in armour.

This is done against a thrust from *posta breve* into *bicorno* to your neck, exactly as shown on f35r.

As your opponent attacks, do the half-sword cover with a *volta stabile,* and then do the half-sword thrust with a pass. N.

Step XIII: *Sottani* applications.

This is done against a *mandritto fendente* to the head from the south.

As your opponent attacks, parry with a false edge *roverso sottano* with one hand, accompanied by a *tornare* of the right foot, and then cut under his arms with a *mandritto sottano*, accompanied by a *passo fora di strada* with your left foot. Follow up with a *roverso fendente* to the head, and then continue through to a rear-weighted *posta di donna destra*. S.

Step XIV: Counterattack, and *stretto* plays.

This is done against a *mandritto fendente* to the head from the south, and is the same counterattack as we see in the Stretto Form of First Drill. Fiore refers to *contratagli*, "countercuts", on f29v, and the pommel strike comes from f30r.

Discrescere offline to *posta di donna destra la soprana* (hands over head); then your opponent attacks. Counterattack with *mandritto fendente* accompanied by a *passo fora di strada*. As the attacker parries, yield, enter with a pommel strike, and pass with your left foot. Follow up with a *mandritto fendente* to *coda longa*, and with a *discrescere* to shorten the stance. S.

Step XV: *Colpo di Villano.*

This is done against a peasant striking an overwhelmingly powerful *mandritto fendente* from the south. F28r.

Grab his blow with *frontale*, with an *acrescere fora di strada*, and allow it to blow through, pushing your blade round in a *molinello*. Strike a *roverso fendente* to his head, with *passo ala traversa* of the right foot. Then pass again, and cover low in *tutta porta di ferro* and *tutta volta*. N.

Step XVI: Blade grab and kick.

This is exactly the fourth play of the Master of the *zogho largo* crossed at the middle of the swords, from f27v, and it is done against a *mandritto fendente* to the head from the north.

Parry with *frontale*. Your opponent's sword remains in reach, so *accrescere* to grab his blade with your left hand and strike a *mandritto fendente* to his head. Kick him just below the knee with your right foot, and then thrust low. Smash his blade into his own neck with your left hand, passing forwards, and thrust high. N.

Step XVII: Withdraw under cover until out of measure.

This is done like part one of the *Farfalla di Ferro*, but passing backwards.

Mandritto fendente with *tornare*; cut through to *fenestra sinestra*, thrust, *roverso fendente* with *tornare*, and cut through to *fenestra destra*. Finish with the sword resting upright on your left shoulder, ready to start again.

The Form, Left-Handed

Step I: Drawing the sword.

This is a defence against dagger attack, as shown on f21v.

Holding the sword and scabbard against your right shoulder, step back offline to your left with your left foot and parry the dagger strike by cutting down from above against the crook of the attacker's elbow. Keeping pressure on the elbow, draw your sword, thrust low and then thrust high in *fenestra la sinestra*. N.

Step II: Sword handling one, from the *Farfalla di Ferro*.

Cut a *mandritto fendente* with a pass through to *dente di zenghiaro*; continue the motion up to *fenestra destra* and thrust with a *roverso punta*. Then turn a *roverso fendente* with a pass through *posta di coda longa* and a *volta stabile* to *posta di fenestra la sinestra*, ending in a rear-weighted stance. N.

Step III: Exchange of thrust.

This is a defence against a thrust to the face. Both attack and defence are from *fenestra sinestra*; this is an application of the ninth and tenth plays of the Master of the *zogho largo* crossed at the middle of the swords, f28v.

Exchange of thrust with an *accrescere fora di strada* and *passo ala traversa*; continue to the hilt grab and disarm (with *meza volta* (left foot) and *tutta volta*), and then thrust low. W.

Step IV: Feint.

This is partly a handling drill. It's the sort of action that is too complex to be likely to work well in combat, but if you can do it at speed or in freeplay then you must have learned some critical skills of timing, tactics and sword handling.

Feint a low thrust with one hand and, as your opponent exchanges, disengage underneath, wind to high one-handed thrust and pass diagonally forward with your left foot. As your opponent parries, yield and cut a *mandritto fendente*, sidestepping with your right foot, ending in *donna destra*. Look over your left shoulder. S.

Step V: *Rompere di punta*, backhand.

This is done against a thrust to the face from *fenestra la sinestra* (creating the same setup with roles reversed that we saw in step one of part two of the cutting drill).

Break the thrust with a *roverso fendente*, with an *accrescere fora di strada* and *passo ala traversa*. End in *tutta porta di ferro*. SSE.

Note, when doing this in a pair drill, you should cut the throat with a *mandritto mezano*. This is elided in the Form with the next step.

Step VI: *Rompere di punta,* forehand.

This is done against a thrust to the belly from *dente di zenghiaro,* and in the normal way.

Breaking the thrust: grab the blade with a *mandritto fendente,* keeping the hands low, and *accrescere fora di strada* and *passo ala traversa;* then cut his throat with a false edge *roverso mezano* to the throat. Follow through with a *roverso fendente* to his head, passing to *tutta porta di ferro.* S.

Step VII: *Rebattere,* forehand.

This is done against a *mandritto fendente* to the head, like in First Drill but with a couple of tweaks.

Parry with *frontale* and cut over his arms with a *mandritto fendente,* with a *passo fora di strada,* and then thrust to chest in *bicorno* with a pass forwards. SW.

Note the *frontale-longa-bicorno* sequence in the hands. Note also the alternative footwork to how we do it in First Drill, and indeed to how Fiore describes the footwork on f27v, where it is the first and second plays of the Master of the *zogho largo* crossed at the middle of the swords.

Step VIII: Master of the sword in one hand.

This is done against a *mandritto fendente* to the head. As you parry, the attacker binds or resists the parry so you cannot beat his sword away and strike, and instead must enter. See f22v.

Lower your sword to the guard of the Master of the sword in one hand, let go with your right hand and look over your shoulder. (NE.)

Rebattere with a true edge *roverso sottano* accompanied by an *acrescimento,* while extending the right hand forward. The attacker resists the parry, so you pass in with a *ligadura mezana* and thrust him in the throat.

Continue with a *mandritto fendente* with a pass (left foot) and *tutta volta,* 135° round, finishing in *dente di zenghiaro.* S.

Step IX: *Rebattere,* backhand.

This is done against a *mandritto fendente* to the head, exactly as in Second Drill. See f33r.

Parry with false edge *roverso sottano* accompanied by an *acrescere fora di strada*, and immediately execute a *mandritto fendente*, which goes through *longa* and through *dente di zenghiaro* and (with a *volta stabile*) to rear-weighted *posta di donna destra*. S.

Step X: Sword handling two.

This is the longest blow in the Art, and the idea is to do it hard and fast and yet be able to instantaneously reverse its direction into a thrust. Good luck.

Roverso fendente with pass to *coda longa*, and immediately thrust to *bicorno* with another pass. S.

Step XI: *Punta falsa.*

This is done against a *mandritto fendente* to the head from the NW. See f29v. Note the alternative footwork, which comes from the defence of the dagger against a sword thrust on f21r, and from the spear guard of *vera croce*.

Parry with *frontale*, with a *tornare* of the right foot, so your opponent's sword is beaten wide. Show him your strong *mezano* to the face with a diagonal sidestep of the left foot (*passo fora di strada*) and, as your opponent parries, execute the *punta falsa* with a pass in with the right foot. NW.

As your opponent parries, throw the hilt of your sword at his head with your left hand shifting to the blade, as in the *Master of Sword-As-Axe*, f24v.

Volta stabile and shift the left foot to face north. Switch your left hand back to the grip so you are now in *vera croce*. N.

Step XII: First play of the sword in armour.

This is done against a thrust from *posta breve* into *bicorno* to your neck, exactly as shown on f35r.

As your opponent attacks, do the half-sword cover with a *volta stabile*, and then do the half-sword thrust with a pass. N.

Step XIII: *Sottani* applications.

This is done against a *mandritto fendente* to the head from the south.

As your opponent attacks, parry with a false edge *roverso sottano* with one hand, accompanied by a *tornare* of the left foot, and then cut under his arms with a *mandritto sottano*, accompanied by a *passo fora di strada* with your right foot. Follow up with a *roverso fendente* to the head, and then continue through to a rear-weighted *posta di donna destra*. S.

Step XIV: Counterattack, and *stretto* plays.

This is done against a *mandritto fendente* to the head from the south, and as the Stretto Form of First Drill. Fiore refers to *contratagli*, "countercuts", on f29v, and the pommel strike comes from f30r.

Discrescere offline to *posta di donna sinestra la soprana* (hands over head); then your opponent attacks. Counterattack with *mandritto fendente* accompanied by a *passo fora di strada*. As the attacker parries, yield, enter with a pommel strike and pass with your right foot. Follow up with a *roverso fendente* to *coda longa*, and with a *discrescere* to shorten the stance. S.

Step XV: Colpo di Villano.

This is done against a peasant striking an overwhelmingly powerful *mandritto fendente* from the south. F28r.

Grab his blow with *frontale*, with an *acrescere fora di strada*, and allow it to blow through, pushing your blade round in a *molinello*. Strike a *roverso fendente* to his head, with *passo ala traversa* of the left foot. Then pass again, and cover low in *tutta porta di ferro* and *tutta volta*. N.

Step XVI: Blade grab and kick.

This is exactly the fourth play of the Master of the *zogho largo* crossed at the middle of the swords, from f27v, and it is done against a *mandritto fendente* to the head from the north.

Parry with *frontale*. Your opponent's sword remains in reach, so *accrescere* to grab his blade with your right hand and strike a *mandritto fendente* to his head. Kick him just below the knee with your left foot, and then thrust low. Smash his blade into his own neck with your right hand, passing forwards, and thrust high. N.

Step XVII: Withdraw under cover until out of measure.

This is done like part one of the *Farfalla di Ferro*, but passing backwards.

Mandritto fendente with *tornare*; cut through to *fenestra destra*, thrust, *roverso fendente* with *tornare*, and cut through to *fenestra sinestra*. Finish with the sword resting upright on your right shoulder, ready to start again.

Got all that? Excellent. Carry on!

As you can see, each step has a specific basic form but can be adapted into all sorts of variations. Each step could represent an entire section of the treatise: the Exchange of Thrusts, for example, might remind you of the spear; the defence against the dagger should remind you of everything you know about the dagger material (you have read *Mastering the Art of Arms: volume 1, The Medieval Dagger*, haven't you?); and so on. In the chapters that follow, I will take you through every step in order and expand on it at length. Let's start with step one ...

Drawing the Sword

This is a defence against a dagger attack, as shown on f21v.

Holding the sword and scabbard against the left shoulder, step back offline to your right with your right foot and parry the dagger strike by cutting down from above against the crook of the attacker's elbow. Keeping pressure on the elbow, draw your sword, thrust low and then thrust high in *fenestra destra*. N.

This is covered in detail in *The Medieval Dagger*, chapter 19, where I take you through all of the plays of the sword against the dagger, and vice versa. But let's take a look at this in more detail.

The sword is in its scabbard, which is being carried in the left hand (and is not attached to the belt). No dagger opponent in their right mind would grab a man holding a sword in its scabbard by the collar and say:

"I will strike you with my dagger before you even draw your sword from its scabbard!"

Nor would the swordsman reply:

"Strike as you will, for I am prepared!"

Though it makes for entertaining and therefore memorable reading.

The lesson here is very interesting. When the sword is held below, it can strike up or down into the attack; when it is held above, it only strikes down. In either case, it immediately controls the weapon and then destroys the man. These plays work best with a rigid scabbard, but they can be done with a flexible leather one as shown here. Medieval scabbards tended to be wood covered with leather, and with a metal tip.

Defence From Above: Down

1. Start with the sword in a scabbard. Hold it with your left hand on the scabbard near the crossguard and your right hand on the handle. The sword points up over your left shoulder. Have your left foot forwards.
2. Daggerman grabs you by the jacket with his left hand and raises his dagger to strike.
3. Drop the scabbarded blade down on his right elbow while stepping back offline to the right (*discrescere*).
4. Draw the sword and thrust to the belly.
5. In the form, we add a second thrust to this: withdraw your sword from his belly, raise it above your shoulder and thrust again.

Mikko grabs Noora by the shoulder, with his dagger raised. Noora steps back offline to her right, striking down over Mikko's arm, and draws the sword, keeping the scabbard in place. She thrusts, and then thrusts again.

This is the basic execution of the play, and it covers the foundations of the Art: control the weapon, control measure and strike when able. From here, you can naturally work backwards through the entire dagger curriculum; this first step locates the sword material in the broader context of Fiore's system. The natural place to go from here is, of course, the dagger section of the manuscript, which I've covered in detail in *The Medieval Dagger*.

Sword Handling One

The thrust at the end of step one finishes in a high one-handed *fenestra* on the right. The next step of the Form continues:

1. turn the sword round the middle of the blade;
2. cut a *mandritto fendente* with a pass through to *dente di zenghiaro*;
3. continue the motion up to *fenestra sinestra* and thrust with a *roverso punta;* and
4. then turn a *roverso fendente* with a pass through *posta di coda longa* and a *volta stabile* to *posta di fenestra*, ending in a rear-weighted stance.

The point of this is to remind you to practise the fundamental skill of sword handling. This sequence is drawn from the *Farfalla di Ferro*, which we went through above.

Ville is in a high one-handed *fenestra* on the right. He turns his sword to strike the *fendente* and passes into *posta longa*, catching the pommel with his left hand. He continues through to *posta di dente di zenghiaro*, and through towards *fenestra sinestra*, arriving in *fenestra sinestra*. He turns round the middle of the blade to strike a *roverso fendente*, passing with the *fendente* into *posta longa*, and arrives in *tutta porta di ferro*. He does a *volta stabile* with the sword's motion towards *fenestra destra*, arriving in *fenestra destra*.

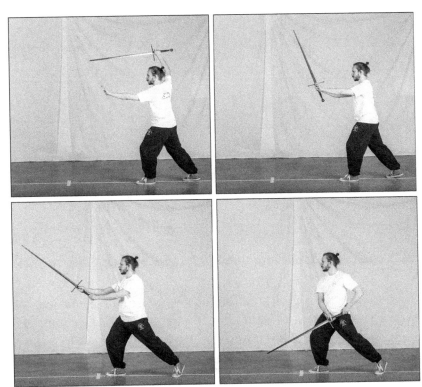

This step of the Form is all about sword handling: making the sword an extension of your arm. Brain scans of carpenters and non-carpenters wielding hammers have shown that the tool is literally treated by the experienced tool user's brain as an extension of their body. I encourage my students to actively think of their nerves and blood vessels creeping down the blade; to think of the point of their sword as the tip of their longest finger. There is no substitute for time spent accomplishing things with the tool for creating this process. You should, eventually, become practically unconscious of the sword, and think only of the target.

Our main tools for this are the pell, the wall target, the buckler and the tyre, all of which we covered in *The Medieval Longsword*. Simply reaching out with the sword instead of just with your hand to make things happen in the world will, over time, make the sword truly part of you. But you absolutely need the targets, as the hammer needs the nail. And of course, the best target is someone's face ...

It is worth taking another look at the grip at this stage. I can usually tell someone's level of training by the way they hold the sword. A newcomer to the Art will begin with a stiff, inefficient and unresponsive grip on the weapon, and over time they will develop a surer, more relaxed and effective way of holding the sword. Let's have a look at how the grip works, and use that to improve our user interface with the weapon.

Every grip requires a fulcrum, a lever and stabilisers. With the longsword, held in two hands, the fulcrum is usually provided by the curled fingers of the sword hand (right for right-handers); the lever is the handle, manipulated by the left hand; and the fingers of both hands keep the sword in the grip, stabilising it. It is useful to think of the grip as a hook (the fingers of the sword hand), which stops the sword from being thrown forwards out of the hand, and a stop (the palm of the other hand), which prevents the sword being rotated out of the hands.

Holding the sword in one hand, we find the middle finger of the sword hand acts as the fulcrum and hook; the heel of the hand acts as the stop. Thus it requires very little grip strength to control the sword.

This critical insight is the single most important factor in developing proper control of the weapon. I usually demonstrate it in class by holding my sword in one hand, leaving my thumb and three fingers conspicuously open, then beating hell out of the tyre and stopping full speed cuts dead an inch above it – all without closing my hand at all.

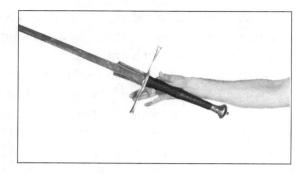

Guy holds the sword with an open hand. The angle seems to show the sword held on my forefinger, but it is actually on my middle finger. However, some of my colleagues prefer to do this on the forefinger. Experiment for yourself.

So lay the handle of your sword along the lifeline of your palm (the crease between the large thumb muscle and the flat of your palm) and gently close your fingers around the grip. Establish that your middle finger and the heel of your palm are in proper contact.

Once this is clear, add your other hand to the pommel, using the palm in the same line as in the sword hand. Gently close the fingers.

Notice that the structure of this grip amply supports the edge and point of the sword, but provides almost no support to the flats. We would need the *bicorno* grip in order to support the flats at the expense of the edges. The function of the grip is to move the sword, and to route energy coming back down the sword – from any impact with the target – safely through your arm and body, and then into the ground.

EXCHANGE THE THRUST

This is a defence against a thrust to the face. Both attack and defence are from *fenestra destra*; this is an application of the ninth and tenth plays of the Master of the *zogho largo* crossed at the middle of the swords, f28v.

You have already seen this done from *tutta porta di ferro* in *The Medieval Longsword*, page 111, so I will not belabour it again here. Fiore's instruction is to step out of the way, pass across and, with your point high and your arms low, cross his sword and strike him in the face or chest. Given that Fiore explicitly states that *fenestra* "knows well the break and exchange", it's reasonable to do it from that guard too.

1. Wait in *fenestra destra*, with the attacker in the same guard.
2. Attacker thrusts to your face.
3. Pick up your point and cross his sword (middle to middle, edge to flat). Your hands should stay low.
4. Step your front (left) foot out of the way.
5. Pass across (so, diagonally left) while thrusting to his face.
6. Reach over with your left hand to grab the opponent's sword between his hands, while passing with your left foot.
7. Turn 90° to your right, swinging your right foot behind you in a *tutta volta*, cranking the attacker's sword anti-clockwise and thrusting to their flank.

As Satu waits in *fenestra*, Henry thrusts at her face. Satu parries with a step offline with her front foot and thrusts through Henry's face, passing across. She reaches over and grabs his sword handle with her left hand, passing with her left foot and turning to her right.

So far, so good. This is a solid basic technique, easily drawn from the treatise. Now what? I would do it all again with a spear.

The Spear

Given the content of Fiore's spear section, it's not unreasonable to think of *fenestra* as a particularly spear-like guard, and the exchange as the quintessential spear technique. So how about going to the treatise, and going through the six guards of the spear and the three plays? They are as follows.

1. Exchange from the right, from all three right-side spear guards: *tutta porta di ferro*, *mezana porta di ferro* and *fenestra*.
2. Counter each of them with the counter-remedy, striking with the butt (*pedale*).
3. Parry and strike from each of the left-side guards: *dente di zenghiaro*, *vera croce* (which will come in handy again when we get to the sword in armour plays), and *fenestra*.

Note that the parry from *vera croce* with a spear is done with a *tornare*, which is an action we will be seeing several times again in the Form.

All of this spear-handling might remind you to practise more with this lovely weapon, and to apply everything you know about weapons-handling practice (see the previous step of the Form) and about using mismatched weapons against each other (see the first step of the Form). Which of Fiore's spear guards is best for defence against a longer weapon? Which guard does he explicitly tell us to use when faced with a sword against a spear?

Notice that in the text of the spear guard *meza porta di ferro*, it says:

> *"Che tutte le guardie che stano fora di strada, cum curta lanzo e curta spada sono sufficinti aspettare ogni arma manuale longa. E quelle de la parte dritto covrano e cum coverta passa e metteno punta. Ele guardi de parte sinstra covrano e rebatteno e di colpo fierano, e non po metter chossi ben punta."*

My translation:

> "That all the guards that are out of the way [by which he means have the point held to the side], with the short lance and short sword are sufficient for waiting all long manual weapons. And those on the right side cover, and with the cover pass and place the thrust. And the guards on the left side cover, and beat away, and strike with a blow, and can not place the thrust so well."

But above the spear guard *dente di zenghiaro,* Fiore states:

> *"Quelle che sono da parte dritta fano qello che fazemo de la riversa. Noy passamo fora de strada inanzi acressando lo pe che denanci come ditto fora de strada. E de nostre punte de parte riversa fazemo derada. E tutte de parte dritta e riversa covegnemo in punta rebatendo finire."*

Translation:

> "Those that are on the right side do what we do on the backhand side. We pass out of the way forwards, stepping the front foot as I said out of the way. And with our thrusts from the backhand side we do damage. And all the forehand and backhand [blows] come together to finish with a battering thrust."

It is clear from the first quote that left- and right-side guards behave differently, but the second quote seems to suggest the opposite. Now it is obvious from the inclusion of both, and from the way that they are grouped here into right-side and left-side guards, that there must be significant differences between them. So I suggest you play around with them and find out what he means for yourself.

While we are at it, let's take another look at the ending of this exchange of thrusts: the tenth play of the Master of the *zogho largo* crossed at the middle of the swords. It allows you to firmly control the opponent's weapon while you hit them. It is also functionally identical to the second play of the Master of the *zogho stretto* where, when finding yourself at the crossing of the *zogho stretto*, you grab the handle of the enemy's sword, passing forwards, and cut or thrust at them. So we could go from here into any of the *stretto* plays, but to my mind the disarms (19th-23rd plays) are the obvious chunk of material to store here. See *The Medieval Longsword*, pages 177-180, for details of how I do them.

THE FEINT

This is partly a handling drill. It's the sort of action that is too complex to be likely to work well in combat, but if you can do it at speed or in freeplay then you must have learned some critical skills of timing, tactics and sword handling. Most specifically: can you manipulate the sword using only your fingers, keeping your wrist still; can you feint without committing to a foot action; can you control the degree of the crossing; can you accurately place a thrust with one hand; and can you effortlessly yield to strike on the other side without even a moment's loss of control?

Here is the drill.

1. You are standing with the sword at your waist, point forward. Opponent is in any right-side guard.
2. Feint a low thrust with one hand.
3. Your opponent tries to exchange your thrust, so disengage underneath, bringing your point back up, and wind to a high one-handed thrust.
4. Pass diagonally forward with your right foot.
5. As your opponent parries, yield and cut a *mandritto fendente*.
6. Sidestep with your left foot at the same time, ending in *donna la sinestra*.
7. Look over your right shoulder. (This last step is just a change of direction.)

Janne feints at Zoë; Zoë attempts the exchange; Janne avoids her blade and raises his blade to parry her thrust. He steps in to thrust at her, which she parries. Janne yields to the parry and strikes Zoë in the head with a *mandritto fendente*.

When we are looking at feinting in Fiore's treatise, we have to content ourselves with hints and suggestions; there is not a single true feint (in which the parry is deceived and no blade contact occurs) in the entire book. The closest is, of course, the *punta falsa*, but in that play Fiore explicitly tells us to "strike lightly on the sword" at the moment that the feint is parried. I cover the basics of feinting on pages 171-173 of *The Medieval Longsword*, and there is no doubt in my mind that when Fiore refers to *posta longa* "avoiding blows" (*gli colpi la schiva*), "using falseness" (*le falsita sa usare*) or *fenestra* being full of deceit (*inganni*), he is talking about actions that we would consider feinting.

Notice that at step seven you change direction for no apparent reason, other than that your next opponent will come from there. Let me give you the real reasons.

1. Control of direction is critically important for the control of measure. What you are learning to do here is to be absolutely consistent and accurate, and to change direction smoothly and precisely.
2. We added this turn to make the Form fit into a smaller space. So far you have been going basically north the whole time; now, with the turn east at the end of the exchange, and with this turn south, you are going back the way you came.
3. None of the basic drills include this kind of limited sidestep with the back foot. But it is useful to be able to do it, so here it is.
4. We wanted to end up in *posta di donna la sinestra* here, and this seemed an efficient way to get there.

But here is the rule, and listen up, this is important. In Form, directions are *absolute* but *arbitrary*. There is not always a good reason (at least, not in other people's Forms; I can justify every direction change in mine) for an action to take place in a specific direction. But one of the greatest gifts of form practise is precision. So be ruthlessly accurate in the directions you are supposed to be going in. 90° is not 89° is not 91°. Got that?

Okay, now let's take a look at the applications to the step. Obviously, go back and revise the basic feinting drills from *The Medieval Longsword,* if you haven't already. Now let's build on that.

Firstly, this feint does not draw a parry: it draws a counterattack. This puts it into a different category altogether. It's much closer to Capoferro (in whose system feints almost invariably incite the opponent to attack) than to most other sources. If your feint draws a counterattack, your next action must be to parry.

Feint draws parry = strike on the other side.
Feint draws counterattack = parry and strike.

In this case you can keep your point free and simply lift your hand
to collect the opponent's point. This is very close to winding (a
term that comes from the Liechtenauer system). In the Italian
canon, we see this kind of action first in Vadi's *De Arte Gladiatoria
Dimicandi*. So here we have a reminder in the Form to go study
your Vadi material and read what he has to say about feints. At
the moment of your thrust, you have collected your opponent's
punta di spada against your *tutta spada*, thus following the age-old
dictum of "strong to weak". Fiore does not discuss this matter of
leverage and the *forte/debole* distinction so beloved of most later
writers, but he does go into it a little in the Morgan MS where, on
f6r, he describes three crossings of the sword:

*"Quista doi magista sono aq incrosadi a tuta spada. Ezoche
po far uno po far l'altro zoe che po fare tuti zoghi de spada
cham lo incrosar. Ma lo incrosar sia de tre rasone, Zoe a tuta
spada e punta de spada. Echi e incrosado a tuta spada pocho
gle po starre. Echie mezo sado a meza spada meno gle po
stare. Echi a punta de spada niente gle po stare. Si che la
spada si ha in si tre cose. zoe pocho, meno e niente."*

Translation:

"These two masters are here crossed to *tuta spada*. And what
one can do the other can do, thus they can do all the plays
of the sword from the crossing. But the crossing is of three
types, thus at *tuta spada* and at *punta de spada*. And the
crossing at *tuta spada* little can it withstand. And *meza spada*
less can it withstand. And a *punta de spada* nothing can it
withstand. And so the sword has in it three things, thus: little,
less and nothing."

Clearly, if you wish to resist your opponent's weapon, you must
put your *tuta spada* in the way of his *punta di spada* for best
results. Fiore, of course, does not usually rely on these more static

parries: he normally advises us to beat the sword away, which necessitates using a faster-moving part of the sword; hence, middle to middle.

You can of course also consider your high thrust as a feint that is parried and, as Vadi advises us in chapter 13, after a feint we should strike on the other side. So this step might be a natural place to store all that you have ever learned about Vadi's swordsmanship. If you haven't learned any Vadi yet, try *Veni Vadi Vici* as an introduction. Don't worry, though, if this seems a little forced to you. There is an actual play from Vadi later in the Form (step twelve).

BREAK THE THRUST, BACKHAND

This is done against a thrust to the face from *fenestra destra*, creating the same setup with roles reversed that we saw in step one of part two of the cutting drill. It is not shown in the Getty MS, but you can see it on carta 21A of the *Pisani Dossi*:

I cover it in detail on page 110 of *The Medieval Longsword*. As a pair drill it works as follows.

1. Wait in *posta di donna la sinestra*; partner is in *fenestra destra*.
2. Partner attacks to your face with a thrust.
3. Break the thrust with a *roverso fendente*, with an *accrescere fora di strada* and *passo ala traversa*, going SSW.
4. Cut his throat with a *mandritto mezano*.

Henry waits in *posta di donna la sinestra*, and Ilpo thrusts Henry in the face; as Ilpo thrusts, Henry breaks the thrust with a *roverso fendente*, stepping his front foot off the line to his right and beating Ilpo's point to the ground; Henry passes across to step on Ilpo's blade and slices Ilpo's throat with a *mezano*.

But in the Form it works as follows when you are working alone.

1. Wait in *posta di donna la sinestra*.
2. Partner attacks to your face with a thrust.
3. Break the thrust with a *roverso fendente*, with an *accrescere fora di strada* and *passo ala traversa*, going SSW.
4. Arrive in *tutta porta di ferro*; go to Form step four.

"What is this?" I hear you cry. "A parry without a riposte? Heresy!" Yes and no. The parry is there and, when you are doing the Form, the beginning of the motion that starts step four (another breaking of the thrust) is identical to the way the sword gets from the end of the breaking *roverso fendente* to the opponent's throat. It makes more sense as a mechanical drill (i.e. one that is supposed to teach you mechanics, ways of moving) to run these together than it would to cut the throat, return to *tutta porta di ferro* and then break the next thrust. This is an embedded lesson in how Forms are put together, and in how actions that are elided in Form may be broken down in several different ways in applications. This allows you, in theory at least, to store more information in less space.

I would recommend that you refer to the *Breaking the Thrust* section in chapter 5 of *The Medieval Longsword*. And while you're at it, why not combine the breaking the thrust exercises with the feint and practise the "Woman in the Window" drill, as well as all the other variations that I cover there.

BREAK THE THRUST, FOREHAND

This is done against a thrust to the belly from *dente di zenghiaro*, and in the normal way (see page 108 of *The Medieval Longsword*).

1. Wait in *tutta porta di ferro*; the attacker is in *zenghiaro*.
2. Attacker enters with a thrust to your belly.
3. Beat his sword down, stepping offline, passing across and keeping your sword forwards, over his.
4. Pick your point up and stroke the tip of the false edge across his throat, keeping your hands low and flicking the point up past his shoulder and across.
5. Continue the motion with a *roverso fendente* to the head. To do this, the point describes a half circle in the air after the throat is cut. Finish facing south.

Jan waits in *tutta porta di ferro*. Zoë thrusts him in the belly from *posta di dente di zenghiaro*. Jan breaks her thrust, catching it with a *fendente*, and drives it to the ground; he passes across to step on her blade and cuts her throat with a *roverso mezano*. Finally, he returns with a *roverso fendente* to her head.

Comparing these two breaks (steps five and six) highlights a principle that is worth paying attention to. When attacking somebody standing in guard, you must bring their sword out along a predictable path so you can get control of it to strike safely. We call this breaking their guard. It has a lot in common with the *obsessio* concept (literally laying siege to someone's guard with a threatening action such as *halpschilt* or *schutzen*) in Royal Armouries MS I.33, and also with the concept of finding, gaining or stringering your opponent's sword in rapier fencing. The defence works in both of these breaks; that's the drill. But you know from either reading *The Medieval Longsword* or from experience that there are many counters to the break; attacking to draw the breaking of the thrust onto your prepared counter-remedy is one way of breaking the defender's guard. But that only works when you don't get hit on the way in: when the only reasonable option they have is to do what you want them to do. One of the rules that governs this is "strike towards their sword". If your opponent is in a high guard, you need to enter with a high attack. If you enter with a low one, your hands (and head) are exposed. The thrust to the belly against *tutta porta di ferro* would get your hands cut off against *posta di donna la sinestra*. Likewise, the high thrust against *posta di donna* exposes your hands if done against a low guard. I recommend putting on a pair of gauntlets and trying this for yourself with a partner who is eager to snipe your hands as you come in.

The 17-20 Drill

So far so good. This can lead us into all sorts of interesting places, not least my current favourite drill based on the basic break: the 17-20 drill. In effect, the *roverso mezano* after the break is countered using the eighteenth play of the *zogho stretto*, which is specifically for countering a *roverso mezano* by "throwing your own *mezano* at his neck". In practice, it works as follows.

1. Attacker starts in *zenghiaro*; defender in *porta di ferro*.
2. Attacker enters with a thrust to the belly.
3. Defender beats his sword down, stepping offline and passing across. Defender also cuts *roverso mezano* to attacker's throat.
4. As the sword comes up, attacker throws his true edge through the flat of the defender's sword.
5. Attacker succeeds in hitting defender in the neck, folding the defender's sword back on his shoulder.
6. Attacker may then enter, grab his own blade with his left hand, and throw.

The next plays in the treatise are the nineteenth and twentieth, which together form the *soprana tor di spada* ("high disarm"). You can find more detailed instructions on how to do this disarm in chapter 9 of *The Medieval Longsword*.

1. Attacker starts in *zenghiaro*; defender in *porta di ferro*.
2. Attacker enters with a thrust to the belly.
3. Defender beats his sword down, stepping offline and passing across. Defender also cuts *roverso mezano* to attacker's throat.
4. As the sword comes up, attacker throws his true edge through the flat of the defender's sword.
5. **But** the defender turns his edge into it and binds.
6. Attacker enters with the disarm from above, wrapping the defender's arms and levering the sword away.

So what about the seventeenth play? Well, it shows a *ligadura mezana* (middle lock) done after the *stretto* crossing, and Fiore explicitly states here that it prevents the disarms ("*Subito fazo questa presa por che ne cum tor di spada ne cum ligadure non mi faza offesa*"); so this can be used to counter the attacker's attempt to do the disarm, as described below:

1. Attacker starts in *zenghiaro*; defender in *porta di ferro*.
2. Attacker enters with a thrust to the belly.
3. Defender beats his sword down, stepping offline and passing across. Defender also cuts *roverso mezano* to attacker's throat.
4. As the sword comes up, attacker throws his true edge through the flat of the defender's sword.
5. But the defender turns his edge into it and binds.
6. Attacker enters with the disarm from above.
7. But the defender extends his left arm, deflects the attacker's wrist and wraps him up.

The Pollax

But wait, there's more! This is the perfect place to start thinking about the pollax plays, because they begin with an illustration of the axes crossed with both heads on the ground. While that does not mean that it shows a breaking of the thrust, in my mind the correlation between the crossings is really obvious. So, how should the pollax be trained?

Firstly, it should be done in armour, but you can and should practise with this lovely weapon even if you don't have your harness yet.

You can start with the *Farfalle di Ferro*, or similar handling drills. Get really comfortable swinging the weapon around. Then try the guards of the axe, which are: *posta breve la serpentina*; *posta de vera croce*; *posta di donna (destra)*; *posta di dente di zenghiaro (or mezana porta di ferro)*; *coda longa*; and *fenestra la sinestra* (which is the only illustration of the left-side *fenestra* in the book).

This is a great section of the book, though it only has eight plays with the axe and two plays after that with trick axes (one with a weight on the end of a rope, and the other with poison dust in a canister attached to the head). Let us leave those two aside for a moment and look at the eight "normal" plays.

First play: the axes are crossed at the ground, and the scholar (note, there is no master in these plays) is left foot forwards; this looks a lot like the breaking of the thrust, and also like the eighth play of the Master of the sword in one hand. But the text can be boiled down to this: beat the axe down if you can and do these plays, unless the opponent counters. Really, that's it. So perhaps we are expected to have read the rest of the book?

Second play: the scholar gets his axe between the player's legs, covers his visor so he can't see and throws him. Getting into this can be tricky, and making it look exactly like the drawing requires some very specific actions on both sides (which we worked out and videoed: Fiore2ndpollaxplay.mov, at https://youtu.be/vOPx0l-C1ZKE).

Third play: stand on the player's axe and belt him in the head. Hmmm, does this sound familiar from the break? If his helmet is getting in your way, go to the fourth play.

Fourth play: open his visor to stab him in the face. We've seen this before in the third play of the sword in armour (which we'll get to later in the Form).

Fifth play: manoeuvre the player into a *ligadura sottana*. This can be quite difficult to do in armour. It's usually much easier to get to push the elbow. But you've done this many times with the sword, and it's not strictly different here. Note also that both the scholar and the player are holding their axes one-handed. This should inspire you to go back and repeat all your axe handling drills again, but one-handed.

Sixth play: disarm. Mechanically, this is just like the 23rd play of the *zogho stretto*, which I covered in *The Medieval Longsword*, pages 177-180. Drop your axe and grab his above and below his hands. I suggest dropping the axe after you have parried, or after your attack has been parried, so his axe is tied up. From the crossing, get one hand on his axe before letting your own drop. Then we have one of the very, very few examples of Fiore's own mechanics terminology used in describing how a play should be done: he tells you to take the axe away with a *meza volta*. Then continue to the next play.

Seventh play: hit your opponent in the head with his own axe. This suggests that the *meza volta*, with which you stripped the axe from his hands in the sixth play, was done with a *tornare*. After mashing his helmet with his axe, go to the eighth play.

Eighth play: grab his visor and throw him to the ground. This is an utterly horrendous throw: the leverage that the visor gives you makes breaking your opponent's neck, well, a snap. So if you are going to do this, be very, very gentle with your partner.

I am well aware that this is not a complete and thorough analysis of the art of murder with the pollax. This excellent and knightly weapon deserves far more space; indeed, perhaps it ought to have a book of its own, such as *Jeu de la Hache*, for example. There is no harm in going through these plays with a dummy axe in t-shirts and masks, but be aware that armour changes everything so you need to be in harness to really get into this. Much will make sense that didn't before. Also, a blunt pollax is called a warhammer. There is no such thing as a safe training pollax that in any way represents the real thing, because if the mass distribution is right then it is at the very least a mallet. Or a sledgehammer. So please be *extra* careful.

PARRY AND STRIKE, FOREHAND

This is done against a *mandritto fendente* to the head, like in First Drill (*The Medieval Longsword*, chapter 7), but with a couple of tweaks and slightly different footwork.

1. Attacker ready in right-side *posta di donna*; you wait in *tutta porta di ferro*.
2. Attacker strikes with *mandritto fendente*, aiming at your head.
3. You parry with a *mandritto sottano* ending in *frontale*, meeting the middle of the attacker's sword with the middle of your own, edge to flat, and beating his sword aside. Attacker's sword is beaten wide to your left, so pass away from it (to your right with your right foot) and strike with a *mandritto fendente* to the attacker's left arm. Shift to *bicorno*, thrusting to the chest while passing in with your left foot. This leaves you facing SE.

Ville waits in *tutta porta di ferro*. Petteri attacks with a *mandritto fendente*. Ville parries middle to middle, striking up into *frontale*, and steps offline with the back foot to strike over Petteri's arms and thrust into his chest with *bicorno*. Ville passes diagonally forwards as Petteri retreats.

Note the *frontale-longa-bicorno* sequence in the hands. Note also the alternative footwork to how we do it in First Drill, and indeed to how Fiore describes the footwork on f27v, where it is the first and second plays of the Master of the *zogho largo* crossed at the middle of the swords.

For the academic case for why we do the play this way, please see my article "One Play, One Drill, Many Questions" online at guywindsor.com.

So where do we go from here? Well, completing First Drill is an obvious development, adding the counter-remedy and the counter-counter-remedy. We can also spend some more time working on grip changes, for which we have an abundance of drills.

Bold and hardy souls with broader fencing interests might even draw a correlation between parrying with *frontale* and using *frontale* as a provocation, and from there find themselves doing sword and buckler drills – specifically besetting Second Ward with Schutzen, as in I.33.

You should be thoroughly familiar with these guards and this play already, so where do we take it from here?

THE SWORD IN ONE HAND

This defence is done against a *mandritto fendente* to the head. As you parry, the attacker binds or resists the parry so you cannot beat his sword away and strike, and instead must enter. See f22v and chapter 8 of *The Medieval Longsword* for detailed instructions.

From the end of step seven:

1. Lower your sword to the guard of the Master of the sword in one hand, let go with your left hand and look over your shoulder. (NW.)
2. *Rebattere* with a true edge *roverso sottano* accompanied by an *acrescimento*, while extending the left hand forward.
3. The attacker resists the parry, so you pass in with a *ligadura mezana* and thrust him in the throat.

Jan waits in the guard of Master of the sword in one hand, and Janne attacks with a *mandritto fendente*. Jan parries with a step offline, beating Janne's sword up and away, but Janne resists the parry. (Note: if Janne did not resist, Jan's sword would end up pointing forwards. Jan is NOT doing a static rising block.) Jan enters with a pass, reaching over Janne's arms, and wraps Janne in a *ligadura mezana*.

If you are doing this on your own, with no partner to get in the way, then:

4. continue with a *mandritto fendente* with a pass (right foot); and
5. then *tutta volta*, 135° round, finishing in *dente di zenghiaro* and facing S.

Note that this continuation does not really work with a partner locked up under your arm, but you can adapt it by putting your sword to their throat and throwing them to the ground in the manner of the tenth play of the *zogho stretto*. For detailed instruction on this, please see my article "8,9,10 Stretto!" It is online and free at guywindsor.com.

This would be the perfect place to go through the eleven plays of the sword in one hand, so let me summarise them for you below.

You parry a cut. It either beats the sword wide or it doesn't. From there, your opponent is either still, moving away or moving in. That gives you the first seven plays; then you have the defence against the thrust, then the defence against an over-committed blow, and finally dealing with an opponent in armour. It looks like this:

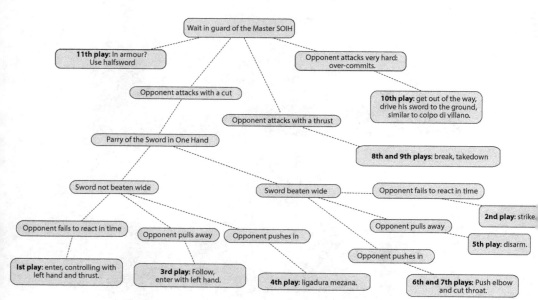

Or indeed, like this:

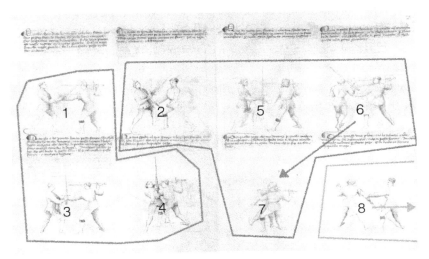

And we turn over the page to see:

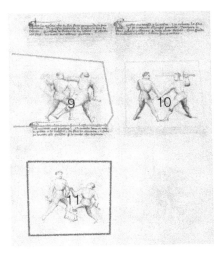

Notice here how we have a complete mini-system that takes into account all eventualities while keeping things very simple. Add the master in all his solo glory and you have twelve plays.

This sort of playing with the arrangement of the material, looking for patterns and looking for ways to chunk things together can make it all much easier to remember; and, of course, it helps you to actually make sense of the material. These are not all separate actions, separate ideas: this treatise is a fantastic, complete and beautifully organised representation of the Art of Arms.

In the Form this step is followed by a very simple action, parrying a *mandritto fendente* with a *roverso sottano* from *posta di dente di zenghiaro*, which in the Getty MS comes at the end of the sword out-of-armour material. So here, in two consecutive steps of the Form, we will have the beginning and the end of the sword; we both start and finish with a parry from the left.

PARRY AND STRIKE, BACKHAND

This is done against a *mandritto fendente* to the head, exactly as in Second Drill. See f33r and chapter 4 of *The Medieval Longsword*.

1. Wait in *zenghiaro* (so, right foot forwards); attacker starts in *donna* on the right.
2. Attacker strikes with *mandritto fendente*.
3. Parry by beating the incoming sword up and to the right with a *roverso sottano* using the false edge, supporting the parry with an *accrescere fora di strada* (a step offline to the right with the front foot).
4. Strike back down the way you came with *mandritto fendente*, bringing your left foot up a bit to return to a normal guard position.
5. If your attacker is imaginary, you can allow the *mandritto fendente* to swing through, letting the momentum carry you into a *volta stabile* and all the way to *posta di donna la sinestra*. You will be facing south.

Mikko waits in *posta di dente di zenghiaro*; Noora attacks with a *mandritto fendente*. Mikko parries with a *roverso sottano*, stepping offline with the front foot and beating Noora's sword away, and strikes with a *mandritto fendente*.

So what are the lessons here? This was the first defence you saw in *The Medieval Longsword,* so we can be pretty sure it's basic stuff. By which I mean *it forms the base of everything you wish to build.* Or, *it is the foundation of your Art.*

So let's review a little. After all this fancy stuff we've done so far, let us remember that this action, as Fiore says on f33r, should be done against all sorts of attacks, and from at least three different guards:

> *"Io spetto questi tre in tal posta, zoe in dente di zengiaro. E in altre guardie poria spettare, zoe in posta de donna la senestra. Anchora in posta di fenestra sinestra cum quello modo e deffesa che faro in dente di zenghiaro. Talmodo e tal deffesa le ditte guardie debian fare. Senza paura io spetto uno a uno e non posso fallire. Ne taglio ne punte ne arme manuale che mi sia lanzada. Lo pe dritto chio denanci acreso for a de strada, E cum lo pe stancho passo ala traversa del arma che me incontra rebatendola in parte riversa. E por questo modo fazo mia deffesa. Fatta la coverta subito faro loffesa."*

Translation:

> "I await these three in this guard, thus: in the boar's tooth. And in other guards I could wait, thus: in the woman's guard on the left; also in the window guard on the left. In this way he who is in the boar's tooth defends himself. This way and this defence the said guards must do. Without fear I await them one by one; and I cannot fail. Neither cut nor thrust, nor any hand weapon that is thrown at me. The right foot that is in front I advance out of the way; and with the left foot I pass on the traverse of the weapon that comes towards me, striking it to the backhand side. And in this way I make my defence. Making the cover I immediately make the offense. (31 recto.)"

Let's make a bullet point list of what Fiore is saying:

- wait in *dente di zenghiaro*;or wait in *fenestra la sinestra* or *posta di donna la sinestra*;
- be not afraid;
- the attackers come one by one;
- the attacks are a cut, a thrust or a thrown weapon;
- step the right foot out of the way and pass across;
- beat the weapon to the *roverso* side (of the opponent – it's mechanically impossible to beat it to your own backhand side from these start positions); and
- strike immediately.

What immediately leaps out at you (or should do so)? Yes, in the application above, we are leaving out the pass across. By what right could we ever do such a thing? It's contrary to the text!

Firstly, we have a documented instance of this exception to the rule in the *Pisani Dossi* manuscript. Here, on carta 14A, the fifth play of the Master of the sword in one hand looks like this:

Which is a lot like the second play as shown in the Getty MS:

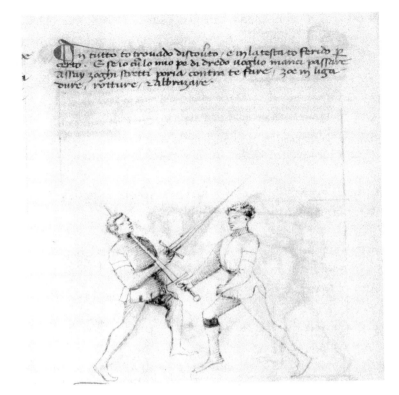

But note! The text in the *Pisani Dossi* clearly states: "*Anchora la testa io ferida senza passare/ Per la bona coverta chio sapuda fare*". Which means: "Again I have struck the head without passing/ by the good cover that I knew to do".

And, if we refer to the text in the Getty MS, though he does not mention footwork, he does begin by saying: "*In tutto to travodo discoverto, e in la testa to ferido per certo*", which means: "I have found you completely uncovered and I will strike you in the head for sure".

Note that in both images the scholar is right foot forwards, and note also that, in the third play of the sword in one hand in the *Pisani Dossi* manuscript, the cut to the head is done with a pass, apparently somewhat to the left.

This suggests to me that if you don't need the pass it is because you have a clear shot at the head and should take it, but it's okay to pass in any case.

And yes, this should flag up for you the fact that the copies of the manuscripts are not identical, and that you must, must, *must* pay attention to all of them. Getty is the base, sure, but without the Morgan we'd have no idea about the *tutta/meza/punta di spada* distinctions, and there is a world of good stuff in the Pisani Dossi too – not least my favourite dagger disarm (the first and second plays of the third master, carta 8B, see *The Medieval Dagger* pages 74-75).

Given that we looked at the pattern of the plays of the Master of the sword in one hand in the Getty MS in the previous chapter, let's take a look at the order in the Pisani Dossi now:

First play: cover and thrust to the chest (on the outside, implying that the parry beat the sword wide).

Second play: thrust with half-sword – though there is no mention of armour in the text, which is odd. Otherwise, it's just like the eleventh play in the Getty MS.

Third play: strike to the head after the cover, and with a pass.

Fourth play: grab the wrist and strike with a thrust on the inside. This is very like the first and third plays in the Getty MS.

Fifth play: this is like the fourth, but it looks like the player is reaching in with his left hand, requiring the scholar to stay a bit further back to get his thrust in.

Sixth play: this is just as the second play in the Getty MS.

Seventh play: disarm, just like the fifth play in the Getty MS.

Eighth play: *ligadura mezana*, done deep, just like in the third play in the Getty MS.

Ninth and tenth plays: push the elbow and cut the throat, just like in the sixth and seventh plays in the Getty MS.

Eleventh and twelfth plays: break the thrust, enter and throw, just like in the eighth and ninth plays of the Getty MS.

Thirteenth play: step on the sword: it looks like the tenth play in the Getty MS, but here the text does not specify that the player has tried to hit the scholar in the head. This may be a development from the breaking of the thrust instead.

It seems to me that the organisation in the Getty MS is much more carefully worked out; I don't see a clear pedagogical pattern in these plays from the Pisani Dossi. Sure, everything is covered, but not in such a systematic way. Also, I find it odd that there would be thirteen plays – and, when you add the master, it even comes to fourteen.

To compound this, let's briefly glance at the Morgan MS. I am 99% sure that this manuscript has been bound in an incorrect order at some stage in the last 600 years, but one thing that doesn't change is the material on each side of a single leaf. Here it appears that the sword in one hand material is immediately followed by the "universal parry" from *dente di zenghiaro*, which is then followed by the defence with staff and dagger against a spear (as it is in the Getty MS), but then we have defence with the dagger against the sword!

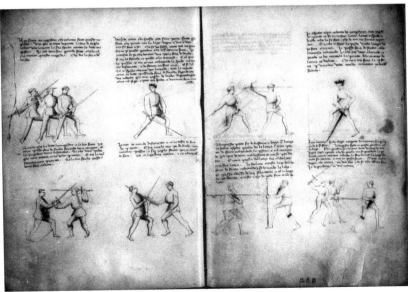

But turn over the leaf and you see that, while the dagger vs. sword material proceeds just like in the Getty MS, on the next page we have what ought to be the last play of the sword in one hand:

While we are on the subject of binding, I hope you recall that the Getty MS itself is not immune. The pages bound in as f40r and f40v (which have the fifth Master of the dagger and some of his plays) manifestly belong between folios 16 (fourth Master) and 17 (which includes the counter-remedy Master to the fifth). I am mentioning this mostly just by way of a warning: if any theory depends too heavily on the ordering of material in a manuscript, it is necessary to establish whether said manuscript is bound correctly.

So, let us get away from academia for a moment and get back to swinging swords. Having worked through all of the plays of the sword in one hand from both manuscripts, and having now thought long and hard about how this material is represented differently between the manuscripts, let's see if the weapon is truly under your control or not.

Sword Handling Two

The *roverso fendente* from a rear-weighted *posta di donna la sinestra*, all the way through to *coda longa*, is the longest single transition between guards in the Art. The idea is to do it hard and fast and yet be able to instantaneously reverse its direction into a thrust. Good luck.

1. Start in *posta di donna la sinestra*, rear-weighted.
2. Strike a fast *roverso fendente* with a pass to *coda longa*. Immediately flip the sword round to thrust into *bicorno* with another pass.
3. Finish facing south.

Henry is in *posta di donna la sinestra* and cuts hard and fast with a *roverso fendente*, passing forwards into *posta longa*. He lets the blow swing on through to *coda longa*, and he immediately flips the sword round and thrusts with *bicorno*, passing again.

The usual error here is to fudge the entry into *coda longa* and instead turn the sword early. Be disciplined, or should I say formal, about going all the way to *coda longa*. You may also find that you are timing your first pass forwards late; you should, of course, be striking a proper *roverso fendente*, which means you should be passing *posta longa* fractionally before the passing foot lands.

But wait! Starting in the rear-weighted guard means that there is ample scope for finishing the first half of the *roverso* during the *volta stabile* that must precede the pass! So how do you time a cut from a rear-weighted guard without getting to the extended position too soon, and without slowing down the weapon so your body and feet can keep up?

Good question. This is one of those moments where I can only say: "welcome to the Advanced class. You figure it out."

Because there isn't one clear answer that works for everyone.

Let me also remind you to check that you understand what I mean by *bicorno*. You can see my interpretation explained in detail on pages 121-125 of *The Medieval Longsword*, and also in my article "Finding Bicorno" (which is up on guywindsor.com).

Now that we're clear on the guard, how do we take the momentum of that mighty *roverso fendente* and use it to fire the thrust forward? Recall that this is a very long blow and that, because the blow has a long way to go, it has lots of time to accelerate, and so it should be moving as fast as it can possibly go. Also, it should go in one direction (straight back, by the end of the blow), but then flip around 180°. The key to it is allowing the sword to pivot within the hand and letting the fast-moving point drag the rest of the sword round.

When beginners are learning the Form, they usually think the *Farfalla di Ferro* is hard, because it has lots of moving parts, and that this exercise is relatively easy, because it is just two blows. But once they understand that the *Farfalla di Ferro* is just a continuous motion machine, its complexity dissolves; this exercise, though, will be hard forever. It never gets easy because its difficulty does not come from complexity, but from challenging the laws of physics.

The Punta Falsa

We have already looked at the basic form of the *punta falsa* in the first section of the book. So what is different here? Well, to start with, we incorporate the *tornare* with the parry, and then we shift the grip to hold the sword like an axe. Let's look at the action as it appears in the Form, and then pull it apart and look at the whys and wherefores.

1. Begin in *bicorno*, facing south. The attack will come from your rear-left quadrant, so from the north-east. As the attack, a *mandritto fendente*, is launched, parry with *frontale*; with a *tornare* of the left foot, bringing it back next to your right foot but not past it. Your opponent's sword is beaten wide.

2. Show him your strong *mezano* to the face with a diagonal sidestep of the right foot (*passo fora di strada*). Your opponent parries; as he does, turn your sword to execute the *punta falsa* with a pass in with the left foot. NE.

3. If your opponent parries, throw the hilt of your sword at his head with the right hand shifting to the blade, as in the Master of sword-as-axe (f24v).

4. To get to the start of the next step, *volta stabile* and then shift the right foot, so you face north, and switch your right hand back to the grip, so you are now in *vera croce*.

Guy waits in *bicorno*; Satu attacks from his rear left side with a *mandritto fendente*. Guy turns with a *tornare* and beats her sword aside. He throws a *mezano* at her face, which she parries. Guy turns his sword and enters with the *punta falsa*. If she parries, Guy throws the hilt of his sword at her head, striking with the crossguard.

Let's take the new bits in order. Where does the *tornare* come from, and why are we doing it not as a full pass but as a kind of gathering of the feet? You can find the *tornare* done with a parry in both the defence of the dagger against a sword thrust on f21r, and with the parry from *vera croce* with the spear on f42r. In the latter case, Fiore explicitly notes that the *tornare* of the front foot is done because the enemy is too close ("*tu me troppo apresso zoga netto. Lo pe dritto che me denanzi in dredo lo tornero*"). The pass back buys you time. Of course, it would buy more time if we did it as a full pass, but here we are only bringing the front foot back towards the other. This is because, in practise, when this is done with the spear and with the aforementioned dagger defence against the sword, a full pass takes you too far away from the opponent to make the strike that the text requires. With the dagger we start right foot forwards and do the *tornare*, and we should then be close enough to enter and strike with a single pass of the left foot; likewise with the spear. If the *tornare* was done like a normal full pass backwards, we could only *accrescere* in with the other foot, or we would have to take a pass forward with the same foot that just passed back (and end up with the wrong foot forward).

In this play we are doing the *tornare* in the same sort of context as with *vera croce* of the spear (the opponent is too close), and we are following up with a pass out of the way to make the *mezano* provocation to set up the *punta falsa*.

So this business of the sword-as-axe. I don't mind telling you that there were some howls of "it's German!" when this was first put to the senior students. Sure, there is a German technique known as the *mortslach* ("murder stroke"), in which you hold the sword by the blade and strike with the hilt, as if it were an axe. So here's the Fiorean take:

This grip is shown on f24v. Fiore says:

"Questa spada sie spada e azza. Egli grandi pesi gli licieri forte impaza. Questa anchora posta de donna la soprana, che

cum le soi malicie le altre gualdie spesso ingana, per che tu crederai che traga de colpo io traro di punto. Io non ho altro a fare che levar gli brazzi sopra la testa. E posso buttar una punta, che io lo presta."

The translation:

"This sword is a sword and an axe. And its great weight makes a strong impediment to lighter [weapons]. This is also the high woman's guard, that with her malice often fools the other guards, because [when] you think that I'll strike with a blow, I strike a thrust. I have nothing else to do but lift my arms over my head. And I can hit with a thrust, with that I am quick."

The sword shown here is a boar sword: a sword with a spear-tip equipped with a secondary crossguard to prevent the enraged and injured boar from charging up the blade and killing you before it dies. You can see examples of this kind of hunting sword in museums; look for a hole in the blade towards the point, through which the second crossguard would be fitted.

Both the pollax and the *punta falsa* are associated with armour (Fiore explicitly states that the *punta falsa* is "*migliore questo zogo in arme che senza*" "this play is better in armour than without".) One reason that Fiore doesn't mention here for holding the sword this way (but which I believe is the case in the German material) is to do damage through armour. The *punta falsa* is of course a deception and, in the text here, this way of holding the sword is done deceptively. You think I'll attack with a crashing great blow of the hilt, but instead I stab you quickly. I do this with the hilt end of the sword, using a quick shift to *fenestra*.

It is very unlikely that you would ever feel the need to shift from the *punta falsa* directly into this grip. As we saw in the Cutting Drill, if your opponent does the proper counter, you're dead already; and if they just parry, the pommel strike will do nicely. But we have included this grip shift here as a reference to armour, to deception and to the boar sword, and as a handling drill.

I've said it before and I'll say it again: the Form is not a choreographed fight; it's a repository for the Art, and adding this odd little grip shift allows us to make all sorts of additional connections and references to the material.

Notice that this step begins with a reference to the spear guard of *vera croce* and ends in the sword in armour guard of *vera croce,* with a technique that is better done with armour than without sandwiched between them. I wonder where we're going with this.

THE SWORD IN ARMOUR

This is done against a thrust from *posta breve* into *bicorno* to your neck, exactly as shown on f35r:

1. Wait in *vera croce*, facing north. Opponent is in *breve*.
2. As your opponent attacks with a thrust, do the half-sword cover with a *volta stabile*. Then do the half-sword thrust with a pass, stabbing him in the face. You are still facing north.
3. To prepare for the next step, look over your right shoulder and let go of the blade with your left hand. You are now facing south.

Noora waits in *vera croce*, and Jan thrusts to her armpit using *bicorno*. Noora sweeps his attack away and enters with a thrust at Jan's face.

The sword in armour is the quintessence of knightly combat on foot. It is a given that the majority of Fiore's students would have done most of their combat, and indeed lived much of their lives, in armour.

But here we have only six guards and just sixteen plays. Compared to the sword *out* of armour, that's nothing! There we have eleven plays of the Master of the sword in one hand; twenty of the *zogho largo*; twenty-three of the *zogho stretto*; twelve guards; and six ways of holding the sword – plus the five sword in the scabbard plays. The answer to this conundrum is in the frequent references to armour throughout the wrestling, dagger and sword plays that precede this. Most of what we have done so far works fine in armour – indeed, some of it works better in armour – and what we have here are the sword plays that you should **only** do in armour. I think of this as the "don't do this without armour" section. Of course when practising the Form, leave it in as a reference to further training; and if you have armour, you should most definitely practice the entire Form while wearing it.

You may have noticed that in this book the attacker's actions are as carefully described as the defender's actions. This is because the actions of the player define those of the scholar: they are the mould in which the scholar's actions are cast. And I have been careful to embed lessons of various sorts into the set-up of most of the steps.

Here, for instance: Fiore explicitly states that *posta breve*, though it is shown in the longsword guards out of armour, is more appropriate when done in armour than without armour (*"E piu e appiada tal guardia inarme che senzarme"*, f26r). So it makes sense to have the attacker do that which *breve* is supposed to do: see if he can enter with a thrust (*"vede se po entrar cum punta"*). And why *bicorno*? It's because the player in the picture looks to me like he is using that guard to strike with.

While we are on the subject of guards, let's take a look at the six guards of the sword in armour.

1. *Posta breve la serpentina*: the short guard of the snake.

2. *Posta di vera croce*: the guard of the true cross.

3. *Serpentino lo soprano*: the high snake.

4. *Porta di ferro la mezana*: the middle iron gate.

5. *Posta sagittaria*: the archer's guard.

6. *Posta de croce bastarda*: the guard of the bastard cross.

There are two snakes, high and short, which both have the point forwards; two crosses, true and bastard, which are both pommel forwards; the archer's guard (point forwards); and the middle iron door, which is held the same in armour as without.

The first two plays show the parry from *vera croce* followed by the thrust. Unusually, in this first play, and in the seventh and eleventh, the defender's starting position (*vera croce*) is explicitly stated. If you'd like some further instruction on how to do the parry, allow me to quote from someone who knew this material far better than I ever will:

> "*E digo de subito zoe come lo zugadore tra una punta alo magistro o scolar che fosse in le ditte guardie overo poste lo magistro lo magistro o vero scolar de anda basso cum la persona e passar fora de strada traversando la spada del scolaro e cum la punta erta al volto overo al petto. E cum lo mantenir de la spada basso, come qui depento.*"

Translation:

> "And I say immediately that the player attacks the master or scholar with a thrust, him being in the said guard or posture; the master, the master or the scholar goes low with their body and passes out of the way, crossing the sword of the scholar and with the point high in to the face or the chest. And with the handle of the sword low, as is shown."

Look at both the level of detail and the errors: those being the repetition of "master", and also his citing the crossing of "la spada del scolaro" (the scholar's sword) when we can tell from the context that it is the player's or opponent's sword that is crossed. But the takeaway (other than that Fiore was human and we must keep our critical faculties engaged when working with the text) is lowering the body and keeping the hilt low. This reminds me a lot of the instructions regarding the exchange of thrusts; there, too, we are told to keep our arms low.

And what of the other plays? Here is a summary.

First and second play: parry and strike from *vera croce*.

Third play: if his visor is in the way, lift it.

Fourth play: when bound at the sword, in the close plays, push the elbow.

Fifth play: if you can't strike with your sword, wrestle: in this case, *a ligadura sottana.*

Sixth play: the completion of the fifth play; note the helmet has fallen off the player. (When I'm demonstrating and I find I have ample time to do a technique, I sometimes refer to writing a letter to my mum before bothering to strike. Here Fiore says: *"Stentar ti posso, ela morte ti posso dare una lettera scriveria che no mello porissi vedare ... "* which translates as: "I can hurt you or give you death, I could write a letter, and you could not even see me ... ".)

Seventh play: parry a thrust from *vera croce* and step in to throw.

Eighth play: having parried, and with the swords now tied up so I can't strike with cut or thrust, I strike with the crossguard or the pommel. This reminds me of Vadi's sword with the sharpened crossguard.

Ninth play: the follow-up to eight: striking with the pommel.

Tenth play: continuing from nine to a takedown.

Eleventh play: parry from *vera croce*, and then counterattack with a thrust. (There is no mention of a parry here.)

Twelvth play: you're in a similar situation to eight, but put the sword round the player's neck and throw.

Thirteenth play: the scholar, again unable to simply strike, jams his point under the player's right arm to get him into an armlock.

Fourteenth play: immobilise the player's sword with your left hand and step behind his front foot to thrust him in the face or throw him.

Fifteenth play: push the elbow. (This is the counter-remedy.)

Sixteenth play: the counter-remedy master has turned to the scholar and now stabs him in the cheeks of the arse, with all due respect! He also notes other potential target areas: in the back, under the arm, in the back of the head, and behind the knees. This is a good reminder of the available targets when in armour.

There is no harm in working all these out from the treatise, but be advised that armour – real armour – changes everything, from your centre of gravity to your perception of threat. So don't take this too seriously or spend too much time on it until you actually have armour. And that's a whole other book …

USING SOTTANI

This is done against a *mandritto fendente* to the head from the south.

1. You are in the guard of the Master of the sword in one hand. Your partner is in *donna destra*, or similar.
2. Partner attacks with a *mandritto fendente*.
3. Parry with a false edge *roverso sottano* with one hand, accompanied by a *tornare* of the right foot. Cut under his arms with a *mandritto sottano*, accompanied by a *passo fora di strada* with your left foot.
4. Follow up by turning your sword around the middle of the blade to strike with a *roverso fendente* to the head, continuing through to a rear-weighted *posta di donna destra* facing south.

Henry waits in the guard of the Master of the sword in one hand; Janne attacks with *mandritto fendente*. Henry parries with a false edge *roverso sottano*, drawing his front foot back (*tornare*); he continues the motion in a *molinello*, striking up at Janne's wrists, passing out of the way and cutting down at Janne's head, and finally bringing his back foot round.

"What?" I hear you cry? "That's not in Fiore! That's from Vadi, or even the Bolognese!"

Well, yes and no. Sure, the flow of this action feels much like some of the Bolognese material, and I freely admit that this is inspired by my reading of Vadi (especially chapter 6, *Veni Vadi Vici*, pp. 61-65). But one of the problems of all book-based swordsmanship is the tendency to copy the lessons without learning them. In other words, to do the actions as set, but not absorb the principles they are intended to embody. I know this because for the last decade I have been coming across readers of my books, some of whom have taken the material and run with it, others for whom the instructions became shackles.

Let's take this *tornare* for example. Yes, there is good evidence to suggest that it is a pass backwards. Fiore suggests as much when he describes the four things in the Art, on f24r: "*passare, tornare, acrescere e discrescere*". But note that in his definition of the *meza volta,* on the same page, he refers to "*un passo o inanzi o indredo*", which is a pass forwards or backwards; so the *tornare* may or may not be "a pass backwards". You already know how I think it should be done in the defence of the dagger against a sword thrust (see *The Medieval Dagger,* pp. 139-141), and with the spear from *vera croce* (see the chapter on the *punta falsa,* page 98). But should this mean that these are the *only* times we should use this very useful step? Some academics would say yes, of course, but no swordsman in their right mind would agree. Fiore gives us two clear examples of what this step does; it is up to us to then use it when necessary.

Parrying with a false-edge *roverso sottano* is a no-brainer if you are in *dente di zenghiaro*. It's a slightly harder sell from the guard of the sword in one hand, because you are apparently chambered for a true-edge *sottano*. But whipping the sword round like that imparts wicked speed and power, especially when accompanied by the *tornare*.

What about this cut to the arms? And from underneath, forsooth! Well, we know from the second play of the Master of the *zogho largo* crossed at the middle of the swords that cutting over the arms is okay after a parry, and that it can be done with a pass out of the way. What if the only open line is from underneath? A purist (and I am one) might shudder to do this, but I say follow the lesson, which is to strike the available targets. Fiore very often has us "give him a good dose of cuts or thrusts" when we have the opportunity. I don't think he'd begrudge us this blow to the arms that simultaneously controls the opponent's weapon and does useful damage.

Returning with a *fendente* to the head is such a common trope in this book that I don't think anyone could reasonably object.

So, do this exercise and make of it what you will. If it's too much interpretation for you, do it as a handling drill or as a preparation for working with Vadi or the Bolognese. But I think the Master would approve.

THE COUNTERATTACK

This is done against a *mandritto fendente* to the head from the south, and as the Stretto Form of First Drill. Fiore refers to *contratagli*, "countercuts", on f29v, and the pommel strike comes from f30r. You can see the basic action on pp. 114-115 of *The Medieval Longsword*, and it is gone into in more depth on pp. 165-180.

1. You are in *posta di donna destra*; your opponent is moving forwards towards any right-side guard from which it is apt to strike a *mandritto fendente*.
2. *Discrescere* offline to *posta di donna destra la soprana* (hands over head) to acquire the desired line and create an opening, into which your opponent attacks with a *mandritto fendente*.
3. Counterattack with *mandritto fendente* accompanied by a *passo fora di strada*.
4. As the attacker parries, yield, enter with a pommel strike and pass in with your left foot.
5. Follow up with a *roverso fendente* to *coda longa*, and with a *discrescere* to shorten the stance. You are facing south.

Ilpo waits in a rear-weighted *posta di donna*, Guy attacks with a *mandritto fendente*. Ilpo counterattacks with the pass out of the way, which Guy parries, and Ilpo enters with a pommel strike that flows into a *roverso fendente* to Guy's head. All the images from this book are available to download free from guywindsor.com, including this sequence shot from the other side, which was omitted from the book by accident.

We should take a moment to look at the idea of the counterattack. We have seen it before in the exchange of thrusts, in the play of the counter to the *punta falsa* and in the eleventh play of the sword in armour. In essence we are talking about parrying and striking, or avoiding and striking, in a single motion. This is in marked contrast to the usual pattern of defence in this system, in which you beat the attack away and then strike. This idea is the foundation of most modern interpretations of the Liechtenauer system, which revolve around the *zornhau ort*, and in essence this action is the same. Against an overhand forehand blow, you step out of the way while making the same blow, which closes the line and puts your point in the opponent's face.

When this counterattack is parried without overcommitment, it invariably looks like the crossing of the *zogho stretto*: middle to middle, points in presence, both players right foot forwards. But if it catches your opponent by surprise, they may very well over-parry, leading you into the idea behind the next play: against overcommitment, strike on the other side. We will go over this in detail in the next chapter.

Notice that, in the basic set-up here, your opponent is moving forward. The point of your *discrescere* is three-fold: it creates an appearance of reluctance to attack, it takes you towards their inside line and it forces them to attack in a longer line. Let's take these in order.

Creating Appearances

One of the key advanced skills any good swordsman must have is the ability to control his opponent's impressions. To literally lay ideas into their mind. The obvious example of this is the feint, which sells them the idea that you are attacking in one line when, in fact, you intend to attack in a different one. Something that Fiore does not address explicitly, but which other masters do, is the idea of making your opponent think you are afraid. In mortal combat, it's probably closer to the truth to think of this as letting some of your fear actually show! Giganti's second book, from 1608, is a case in point: when defending with just a dagger against a spear, you are supposed to make the spearman think you are scared in order to incite him to attack with less caution and onto your ready defence. Perhaps the most famous example of this in British history is the Battle of Hastings, in 1066. The Norman cavalry under William (soon to be called William the Conqueror) charged several times against the Saxon shield wall, commanded by Harold.

This was going to go on all day, and the Saxons on their hill would have probably been just fine. But Harold got an arrow in his eye and so lost command, and William ordered his men to charge again, then appear to run away in disorder. As they did so, the Saxons broke their wall and chased after them, bent on slaughter (in pre-modern battle, the majority of casualties on the losing side usually occurred after they had turned to run away). At which point, the Normans rallied, turned again, and destroyed the Saxons piecemeal. Their retreat was a stratagem designed to lure the Saxons out of a strong defensive position. The skill comes in two parts: the ability to sell the retreat as genuine and the ability to reverse the retreat. It is axiomatic in military lore that any army can attack; it takes a great one to retreat under cover with minimum losses. It is also axiomatic that it is much harder to change direction than it is to keep going.

At the end of this step you prepare for the next one with another *discrescere*, this time straight back. Its function is to again create an appearance of reluctance, and also to disguise the shortening of your stance. The step back of the right foot is of the normal length; the step back of the left (front) foot, to regain your stance, is a bit longer. We will look at why in the next chapter.

The lesson of the *discrescere* here is that you must be able to sell an opening, and also be able to change direction at speed and under pressure. You will not learn this from this step alone but, if you have been paying attention and diligently studying the materials in front of you, I have no doubt that you can work out a training regime for acquiring both these skills.

Control the Line

By stepping to your right against an opponent who is chambered on their right, you naturally acquire a better line in which to strike. We see this all over the place, but often after a parry. The second play of the Master of the *zogho largo* crossed at the middle of the swords is a good example. By doing this early, and so before the attack is actually launched, we can make the counterattack easier for us.

This goes both ways, of course. Try this: put your partner on guard on their right. Attack with a *mandritto fendente* to their head in three different ways: with an absolutely direct pass forwards; then passing a little to your right; and then passing a little to your left. When you attack slightly offline to your right, it is easier for you mechanically, but it leaves you more open to the counterattack. Not coincidentally, it also means that their parry – if they make one – has farther to go (they are chambered on their right, and your blade is coming farther over to their left), so is easier to counter. When you attack slightly to your left, you close off the line of the counterattack, but their parry has less far to go.

This ability to strike in such a way that the counterattack would fail, if it's made, has led to the idea in some students of "cutting into the crossing". This presupposes that the counterattack will always be attempted, even when it is doomed (I hope it's obvious that counterattacking into a closed line is a mistake). I abhor this notion, and ask you to delete it from your vocabulary. You cut into your opponent's head, taking into account his likely actions. But you never deliberately cut to create a crossing. Yes, you might attack to draw out his weapon so it can be dealt with, but the crossing is *never the destination*. So you cut at the target; or you cut through his parry; or you cut to draw his counterattack onto your prepared parry, and then strike; or you cut in such a way that you can predict, and thus take advantage of, the crossing that will occur; or somesuch. But never, ever, aim for the crossing. Crossings don't win sword fights.

Both of these offline options, being slightly indirect, cost you some measure in exchange for a greater ability to predict your opponent's likely actions. Attacking up the zero line, neither right nor left, almost never happens outside of basic drill. The reason we include it there is that it is much easier to spot deviations from precision when you are intending to be on the direct line. Once you have developed precision, you can apply it to whatever line you feel most useful. It has been my experience that the principle difference between proper schools and study groups is the level of precision the students attain: I have seen legions of swordsmen who couldn't do the same action exactly the same way twice. They will sometimes try to defend this as making them unpredictable and thus harder to fence against; I would suggest that while it's good to be unpredictable from your opponent's perspective, it is woefully short-sighted to think it's a good idea to be unpredictable to yourself. This idea of being precise when it comes to direction is of course embedded at the deepest possible level in the Form. Every action is done in exactly the set direction only, until control of direction is built into you.

Extend the Line

By stepping offline, instead of straight back, you increase the distance between your head and his sword, and so force your opponent into a longer line. This takes him more time to cover, which is time that you can use for your defence. Measure is time, after all.

But here is the trick: by aligning yourself towards your opponent, you maximise your reach; but if he is organised towards where you were, his reach is compromised. You have seen this already in the second step of First Drill (aka the second play of the Master of the *zogho largo* crossed at the middle of the swords); if you step exactly as set, you end up able to thrust into his chest while he cannot reach you without taking another step. This is simple geometry.

Your *discrescere* offline here is taking you away from his line of maximum strength and reach. He has to change direction slightly to attack you. In this change of direction he signals his intentions and is simultaneously walking into your prepared trap. Really, there is no excuse for your counterattack to fail!

So where do we go from here? The obvious place, to my mind, is variations on your response to his parry. If you anticipate it well enough, you can deceive it and strike on the other side. Or you can go to the twelfth play of the *zogho stretto*, f31r, where Fiore says:

> "*Se uno se covra dela parte dritta, pigla cum la tua mane stancha la sua spada per questo modo, e fierlo di punta voy cum lo taglio.*"

Translation:

> "If one covers from the forehand side, grab with your left hand his sword in this way, and strike him with a thrust or with the cut."

I take this to mean "when the opponent parries from the forehand side", because the illustration clearly shows you hitting him in the neck with his own sword. This happens easily if his blade starts out on your right (as it does if he is parrying); if you have parried from your *mandritto* side, your sword is on your left and his is on the far side of it. Grabbing it in those circumstances would lead you into the third or fourth play of the Master of the *zogho largo* crossed at the middle of the swords, which we will cover in a later chapter. This, of course, is yet another data point in favour of my thesis regarding the meaning of *largo* and *stretto*, as discussed on pages 43-45 of *The Medieval Longsword*.

The Stretto From of First Drill

Other variations would include the disarms (19th-23rd plays of the *zogho stretto*). You can of course take the *stretto* form of First Drill as your base for further work. The key to that drill is the branching: at the moment of the crossing, either player can act. The actions are described on pages 165-170 of *The Medieval Longsword,* but the drill itself is not, so I'll include it here. From the point where the counterattack is parried, the attacker can continue with the second play of the *zogho stretto* or the defender with the third, depending on who is ready for it first. In part one, the attacker enters at the crossing, to which the defender has a counter; in part two, as the crossing is made, the defender enters, which is a move that the attacker has a counter against.

So the *stretto* form of First Drill, part one, goes as follows.

1. Both players are in *posta di donna destra*. The attacker initiates with a *mandritto fendente*.
2. The defender counterattacks, also with a *mandritto fendente*, sending his point into the attacker's face.
3. The attacker parries the counterattack, keeping his point close to the defender's face, and grabs the defender's hilt (as in the second play of the *zogho stretto*).
4. As the attacker parries, the defender grabs the attacker's point and smashes his sword into his face (the twelvth play of the *zogho stretto*).

The *stretto* form of First Drill, part two, goes as follows.

1. Both players are in *posta di donna destra*. The attacker initiates with a *mandritto fendente*.
2. The defender counterattacks, also with a *mandritto fendente*, sending his point into the attacker's face.
3. The attacker parries the counterattack, and the defender enters with a pommel strike (third play of the *zogho stretto*).
4. The attacker counters the pommel strike with the *ligadura mezana*.

The Stretto From of Second Drill

This may beg the question, "what about Second Drill?" To which I say: do you remember the plays of the Master of the sword in one hand? Step eight, in which the attacker bound the parry and prevented the riposte, so that you had to enter? We do, of course, have a *stretto* form of Second Drill, which models what happens when a parry from the *roverso* side works but does not beat the attack wide. In this instance the attacker binds the parry and enters with a version of the (Getty MS) eleventh play of the *zogho stretto*. The defender prevents this with the play of the second Master of the *zogho stretto* (Pisani Dossi MS), who has crossed from the *roverso* side.

The *stretto* form of Second Drill, part one, goes as follows.

1. The attacker initiates with a *mandritto fendente*.
2. The defender parries with a *roverso sottano* and strikes with a *mandritto fendente*.

3. As the defender parries, the attacker binds the parry, grabs the defender's pommel with his left hand, and throws it over the defender's left shoulder (the eleventh play of the *zogho stretto*).

4. As the attacker binds and tries to enter, the defender kicks him in the nuts (stomach, amongst friends), and then strikes with the sword.

The *stretto* form of Second Drill, part two, goes as follows.

1. The attacker initiates with a *mandritto fendente*.

2. The defender parries with a *roverso sottano* and strikes with a *mandritto fendente*.

3. As the attacker binds the parry, the defender enters to wrap (as we see, for example, in the Pisani Dossi MS, first and second plays of the second Master of the *zogho stretto*).

4. The defender counters the *ligadura mezana* with the sixteenth play of the *zogho stretto* (Getty MS). Note we already have the fifteenth play as a counter to the *ligadura* in the base form of Second Drill, so here is the alternative.

Alert readers are right now jumping up and down in their seats: "you mean there is another Master of the *zogho stretto*, who covers from the left side, in the Pisani Dossi but not in the Getty?" Yes, I do, and it's really interesting …

The text above the Master reads:

Questa e coverta de la riverssa mano
Per far zoghi de fortissimi ingano

Translation:

"This is a cover from the backhand side,
To make plays of maximum deception."

And his first scholar's text reads:

Per la coverta de la riverssa mano acqui to afato
De zogho streto e de ferite non sera guardato.

Translation:

"By the cover of the backhand here I have done to you,
You cannot protect yourself from the constrained play and
the strikes."

This Master is the thirteenth play of the *zogho stretto* in this manuscript, and he is followed by two scholars and a counter-remedy Master
before the action switches back to the *mandritto* side. This presents
a really interesting organisational problem: this Master appears in the
midst of the scholars of the previous Master. Because his plays cover
only one side of the folio (carta 23B), we can be reasonably sure that
this is not a binding mistake. Text with the subsequent scholar, on
24A, begins *"Per la coverta de man drita ... "* ("by the cover of the
forehand side ... "), which suggests that the writer was aware of the
possibility for confusion. But my point here is that, as you can see
from the images, the parry has succeeded (the Master doesn't have a
sword in his head), and the opening he finds is on the inside. So the
player's sword must be moving (or applying pressure) to the Master's
left. If this play began (as it appears to) with the player attacking with
a *roverso fendente* towards the Master's head, the only way for this
situation to occur as shown is for that attack to be diverted away from
the head and towards the Master's sword. Otherwise the parry would
have beaten the attack wide and the Master could simply strike (as in
the second play of the Master of the sword in one hand).

THE COLPO DI VILLANO

This is done against a peasant striking an overwhelmingly powerful *mandritto fendente* from the south. It's shown in the Getty MS at f28r. At the end of the previous step you deliberately shortened your stance with a *discrescere*. This is because Fiore explicitly tells us in the text for this play that *"quello che lo colpo aspetta de stare in picolo passo cum lo pe stancho denanzi"* ("the one that waits for the blow should be in a 'small pace'" – i.e. a narrow stance, with the left foot forwards). You can find the basic instructions on page 153 of *The Medieval Longsword*. As always, make sure that the basic form of the drill is comfortable before you add it to the Form.

1. Await the peasant's blow in *coda longa*. Opponent is in *posta di donna destra*.
2. Opponent comes to strike with a *mandritto fendente*.
3. Parry, sweeping your sword up into *frontale*, and meet his sword in the middle.
4. Step to your left, out of the way, with the front foot.
5. Pass across with your right foot.
6. Let his sword push yours round in a *molinello* and let his slide off to the ground.
7. Strike him with a *roverso fendente*.
8. He pulls back.
9. Follow him with a pass forward with the left foot, and bind his sword from above.
10. Let the momentum of the *roverso fendente* carry you round in a *tutta volta*, to end in *tutta porta di ferro* facing north.

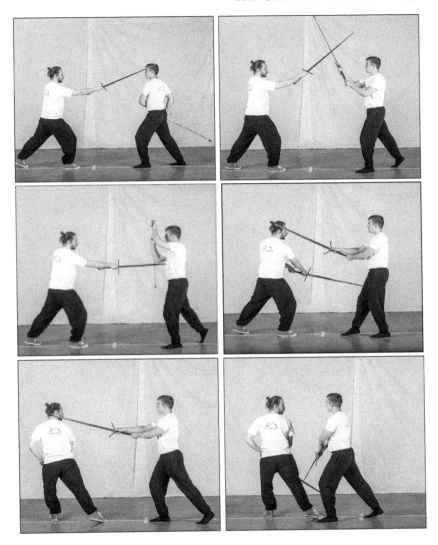

Jan waits for Ville's blow in *coda longa*. As Ville attacks, Jan parries, stepping off the line with his front foot, yielding to Ville's force and striking on the other side with a pass across. As Ville pulls away, Jan follows him and covers Ville's sword with his own.

Let's have a look at Fiore's instructions. I often quote this passage when someone asks me whether it's possible to recreate the Art accurately. Students of other masters, especially medieval masters, are usually very jealous of the level of detail Fiore gives. I tell them it's not too late to convert to the TRUE religion:

> *"Questo zogho sie chiamado colpo di villano, e sta in tal modo, zoe che si de aspettare lo villano che lo traga cum sua spada. Equello che lo colpo aspetta de stare in picolo passo cum lo pe stancho denanzi. Esubito che lo villano ti tra per ferire*

THE COLPO DI VILLANO ✦ 129

acresse lo pe stancho fora de strada inverso la parte dritta.
Ecum lo dritto passa ala traversa fora di stada piglando lo
suo colpo ameza la tua spada. Elassa discorrer la sua spada
aterra e subito responde gli cum lo fendente per la testa overo
per gli brazi, overo cum la punta in lo petto come depento.
Anchora e questa zogho bon cum la spada contra la azza, e
contra un bastone grave o liziero."

Translation:

"This play is called the peasant's blow, and it is like this, so,
one waits for the peasant that he strikes with his sword. And
the one who waits for the blow should be in a narrow stance
with the left foot forwards. And immediately that the peasant
comes to strike advance your left foot out of the way towards
the forehand side [of the peasant; going to your right does not
get you to the other side of his sword as the images show and
the text will imply]. And with the right foot pass across out of
the way, catching his blow in the middle of your sword. And
let his sword run off to the ground and immediately respond
to it with a *fendente* to the head, or to the arms, or with a
thrust in the chest as is shown. Also this play is good with the
sword against the axe, and against a stick, heavy or light."

In the Pisani Dossi, the instructions for the same play (which occurs
in the same place: fifth and sixth plays of the Master of the *zogho
largo* crossed at the middle of the swords) are a little different:

Per passar fora de strada io to ben discoverto
E li braci toy io si feriro in lo voltare presto

Translation:

With the pass out of the way I have uncovered you
and in the quick turning I will strike your arms.

Compared to the Getty MS this is woefully unhelpful, but compared
to most other contemporary treatises it is a miracle of clarity. A

great and unexplored thesis in medieval martial arts is the incredible differences in the sophistication; not in the swordsmanship, but in the way it is represented on the page.

One of the details I am particularly struck by in the Getty version is the verb "pigliare", to catch or grab, to describe how the blades meet. It is very different to "rebattere", to beat away. He uses the same verb in the instructions for the *rompere di punta* on f28v: *"che lo scolaro va cum gli brazzi erti e pigla lo fendente cum lo acresser e passare fora de strada e tra per traversa la punta quasi ameza spada a rebater la a terra".* ("The scholar goes with the arms high and grabs [with] the *fendente* with the step and pass out of the way and strikes across the thrust about at the middle of the sword and beats it to the ground.")

Notice that I am using the term "instructions" regarding Fiore's text, as if they were somehow meant to teach the Art. Some would have it that they are descriptions, not instructions: "this is how it is done" not "this is how you should do it". I would argue that in the introduction he makes it perfectly clear that you are supposed to be able to learn the Art from this book. Yes, he assumes that you are of the right class, and therefore have a solid background in knightly martial arts, but he says at the end of his introduction:

> *"E questo intende solamente por che chosi bisogna esser guardie e magistri in le altre arte e rimedii e contrarii come in larte de abrazare azo che lo libro si possa liceramente intendere. Ben che le rubriche e le figure, e li zoghi mostrarana tutta larte si bene che tutta la si pora intendere. Ora atendemo ale figure depinte e alor zoghi e aloro parole le quale ne mostrara la veritade."*

Translation:

> "And this means only that you need to have guards and masters in the other arts, and remedies and counters as in the art of wrestling such as the book can be easily understood. Well, the rubric and the figures and the plays show all of the art so well that anyone could understand. Now we pay attention to

the drawn figures and to their plays and to their speech, which show us the truth."

This strikes me as a pretty clear indication that the author's intention is that this book is sufficient to represent the Art completely, given his natural assumptions about his readership. But is it *instructional* or *representative*? The verb *"mostrare"*, to show, implies the latter, I think; but to pick one of the many examples, in the text above the Master of *coda longa* on horseback (f45v), Fiore says:

" ... *E tente ben a mente che le punte e li colpi riversi si debano rebatter in fora, zoe, ala traversa e non in erto. Eli colip de fendenti si debano rebatter per lo simile in fora, levando un pocho la spada dello suo inimigo ... .*"

Translation:

" ... And keep well in mind that thrusts and the backhand blows should be beaten away, so, across and not up. And the downwards blows must be beaten similarly away, lifting a little the sword of your enemy ... ."

That sounds like instruction to me.

Speaking of which, what are the lessons of this play? To my mind, the key component is the idea that against overwhelming force you should yield and strike on the other side. This is a martial arts truism, so how should it be applied? In essence, one of the key distinctions we have to make in this art, between *largo* and *stretto*, is often misapplied because of a lack of sensitivity to the lesson of the *colpo di villano*. I have lost count of the number of missed opportunities to strike that I have seen in freeplay because one player failed to see that their opponent was binding their sword too hard, and therefore were vulnerable to a strike on the other side.

For instance, let's hark back to the previous step, which involves the *stretto* form of First Drill. When done at speed, it is very, very common for the attacker, being counterattacked, to over-parry, letting their sword go too far across. In that circumstance, the most efficient continuation for the defender is to strike on the other side with a *fendente*, rather than follow the drill and go to the pommel strike. You could easily set that up as a coaching drill in either direction: the defender parries or counterattacks, so the attacker can practise a controlled parry before her entry; or the attacker can train the defender to notice when she randomly over-parries, in which case he should strike on the other side. In each case, of course and as always, if the student gets it right, they strike, and if they get it wrong, their action must fail.

You might also want to go back to the "exchange the thrust" drill, step three, because it is very common for the scholar to take her point offline on the entry after the exchange, when really it should remain threatening all the way in. The player (the one who attacked with a thrust and has been exchanged against) has far more options to counter when the sword is *not* in their face.

BLADE GRAB AND KICK

This is exactly the fourth play of the Master of the *zogho largo* crossed at the middle of the swords, from f27v, and it is done against a *mandritto fendente* to the head from the north. It is followed by the twelvth play of the *zogho stretto* (which you have already seen in the expansion on step fourteen), because one of the key goals of the Form is to teach you to **keep moving**. If you refer to my article on the eighth, ninth and tenth plays of the *zogho stretto*, you'll see an example of how you smash their weapon away, wrap them up, hit them repeatedly with your sword and then throw them to the ground. You do not, must not, simply tag them with your weapon and count the fight as done.

Anyway, without further ado ...

1. You are in *tutta porta di ferro*. Your opponent is in *posta di donna destra*.
2. Your opponent attacks with a *mandritto fendente*.
3. Parry with *frontale*, as per the Master of the *zogho largo* crossed at the middle of the swords.
4. Your opponent's sword remains in reach, so *accrescere* to grab her blade with your left hand. Strike a *mandritto fendente* to her head.
5. Kick her just below the knee with your right foot, and then thrust low.
6. Smash her blade into her own neck with your left hand, passing forwards, and thrust her in the face.
7. Pass back, cutting her head with a *mandritto fendente*. You are facing north.

Zoë waits in *tutta porta di ferro*; Ilpo attacks with *mandritto fendente*. Zoë parries. Ilpo's point remains in reach, so she steps offline with her front foot, grabs his point and cuts at his head. She kicks him below the knee, thrusts him in the belly, smashes his blade into his neck and stabs him in the face. She then releases him, passes back and cuts him in the head.

The general rules are as follows.

- Parry.
- If you can grab the blade, you should.
- Step as needed.
- Kick only when the opponent's blade is occupied and there is no pressure towards you.
- Keep moving, keep striking.

Let's take them in order and look at them in more detail.

There can be no doubt that the default defensive action in this system is the parry. Many of the plays occur when the parry has succeeded well enough that you have not been hit, but you cannot strike directly. The exceptions are the second plays of the following Masters:

- the Master of the sword in one hand,
- the Master of the *zogho largo* crossed at the points of the swords,
- the Master of the *zogho largo* crossed at the middle of the swords, and
- the Master of the sword in armour.

I see a pattern here: the Master shows the parry and his second play is the strike following a successful parry. There is also the parry done from *dente di zenghiaro* after the *stretto* plays, with no illustrated plays following it. The apparent exception to the pattern would be the sword in one hand section, where the first play is a scholar of the Master, so the second play does actually follow the pattern.

That is 5 plays out of 70. Which is about right, I imagine, given that most of the time the attacker has plans of his own that take your rather predictable parry into account.

The fundamental principle of controlling your opponent's weapon is never clearer than when you literally grab it. It's interesting to note that Fiore thinks it is important enough that he shows it twice here (third and fourth plays), done both without the kick and with it. It is also important and useful enough to be worth stepping for – Fiore explicitly tells us to step forward (*"acresser inanzi"*) to grab.

Kicking is one of those often overlooked aspects of medieval martial arts. Kicks are not terribly common. Fiore shows one knee to the balls on f9v, this kick on f27v and the kick to the balls on f28r. That's it. In each case, they are not usually fight-finishers. They are intended to weaken the opponent long enough to allow you to do other things (the one on f27v may be an exception, as it *"guastar la gamba"*, or "ruins the leg", but the image clearly shows a strike with the sword happening at the same time).

Notice, incidentally, that if you are crossed in the *zogho stretto*, lifting one foot off the ground should weaken you sufficiently that your opponent's weapon ends up in your face. Try it with a friend, not an enemy.

This might be a good place to look at kicking in general. I include a basic kicking curriculum in the core syllabus because they are a part of Fiore's system, even if only a small part, and if we are going to train these actions safely, you must be able to kick under complete control.

Basic Kicking

For many of my beginner students, standing on one leg is a challenge, and kicking even more so. The main challenges are balance, flexibility and strength. We deal with all of those by doing lots of slow, careful kicks. I think it is necessary for anyone who calls themselves a martial artist to be able to kick, punch and grapple, and to be handy with sticks and with bladed weapons of every common length. Within those areas, one will tend to specialise (I am a relatively weak grappler, for instance), but basic training should create a broad and stable base, covering all of the above, whatever your style or specialty.

What follows then is a brief overview of our core kicking curriculum, which is intended to provide you with sufficient kicking skill to use Fiore's kicking plays, and a basic understanding of how kicks work. There is, of course, a video on the wiki that covers all of this.

In all of these exercises that follow, remember the points below.

- Go slowly: get the kick smooth, supported and balanced before adding any power at all.
- It's all about support: every kick in the basic syllabus should create a groundpath between your kicking foot and your supporting foot.

Your supporting foot will always be aligned in the direction of the forces acting on the kick. If the kick goes forwards, your supporting foot will be on the same line. If the kick goes across, your supporting foot will also be going across.

In Fiore's Art, kicks are only done when your hands are busy and you are in physical contact with your opponent (the swords may be crossed, for instance). This means that your hands are doing something useful, and that these kicks involve no reciprocal action in the upper body. This is unlike most other kicking arts, where you can generate extra power by leaning back with the torso or by using your hands in some way. To start with, in every case, keep your hands still and your torso upright, unless specifically told otherwise.

Let's start with the front kick.

The Front Kick
1. Start on guard, left foot forwards.
2. Pick up your right knee as high as it will go.
3. Quite slowly extend your right foot, heel first, as high as you can comfortably hold it. Think "thrust".
4. Your supporting foot will turn a little, but must remain flat on the ground.
5. Place your right foot down in front of you, creating a new guard position.
6. Repeat for the other side.

Guy stands on guard, raises his right foot with the knee
high, and extends the leg forwards through the heel.

As a groin kick, think of using the sole of your foot to crush his
testicles against his pelvis like crushing grapes against a wall. If
you are strong enough and flexible enough to aim for the stomach,
then point your foot forwards, pull your toes back and kick with
the ball of the foot. Practise both striking surfaces of the foot,
regardless of how high you can reach, so that you are used to them
when you *can* place your foot at any height.

Can't kick higher than your own knee? No problem. The limiting
factor is either muscular stiffness, inhibiting the movement, or lack
of strength in the key areas. I'll deal with that in detail in another
book but, for now, just gently work on the exercise and your kick
will improve.

You must never kick higher than the height at which you can
hold your foot out for at least ten seconds. We are not interested
(at this stage at least) in swinging the foot ballistically. If you want

to kick someone in the head, break their knee with your first kick: when they fall down their head will be at a convenient height for you.

During the photoshoot for this book we realised that we were in danger of producing a book of mine with no groin kick. This would be catastrophic, so Zoë kindly volunteered to hoof Ilpo in the nuts. This is the eighth play of the Master of *zogho largo* crossed at the middle of the swords:

Zoë parries Ilpo's attack, steps forward and kicks him in the nuts. She finishes him off with a cut to the head. You can find the counter in *The Medieval Longsword*, p. 157.

The Round Kick

I tend to use this kick against the side of the knee, the floating ribs and, if I'm off to the side, the stomach. The key to this kick is hiding it. It begins exactly like the front kick.

1. Start on guard, left foot forwards.
2. Pick up your right knee as high as it will go.
3. As you extend the leg, pivot your left foot on the ball, 90° anticlockwise, while turning your right leg so that it strikes across. Think "*mandritto mezano*".
4. Place the foot down in front of you. If you have any doubts about control, return it to the start position.
5. Repeat on the other side.

Jan raises his knee, pivots his hips and his supporting foot, and kicks around.

In some arts, this kick is done with the ball of the foot. I have never managed to get my feet flexible enough to do that. I strike with the top of my foot – with my shoelaces, if you will. If I am too close for that, I use my shin.

With a bit of practise this becomes a natural, relaxed, flail-like motion where your lower leg hinges at the knee like a pair of nunchaku. But be careful to build this up slowly, because you can easily end up hurting your knee by snapping this out too vigorously too soon.

The Side Kick

This kick will almost never be used from a normal, forward-facing guard position straight in front of you. But we do it that way in basic practice because it's a useful test of control and precision. Let's build up to that.

1. Stand normally, with your feet a bit wider than your shoulders.
2. Look to your right, over your right shoulder.
3. Lift your right knee as high as you can.
4. Extend your right leg, leading with the edge of your foot, exactly to your right and in line with the line between your feet.
5. As you extend, turn your left foot 90° anti-clockwise so that your heel is pointed to the right.
6. Recover back the way you came.

When this is comfortable on both sides, try the following.

1. Start on guard, left foot forwards.
2. Pick up your right knee as high as it will go.
3. As you extend the leg, leading with the edge of the foot, pivot your left foot on the ball, 180° anticlockwise.
4. This is accompanied by a slight lean backwards in the shoulders.
5. Place the foot in front of you.

Guy raises his knee, pivots his hips and supporting foot, and extends his leg sideways, striking with the edge of the foot.

All Three Together

This is my go-to exercise for maintaining my kicking skills without spending too much time on them. We will do all three kicks in one go, and without putting the kicking foot down. Get comfortable with the kicks individually before you try this.

1. Start on guard, left foot forwards.
2. Pick up your right knee as high as it will go.
3. Do the front kick.
4. Bring the foot back, keeping the knee high.
5. Do the round kick, pivoting your left foot on the ball, 90° anticlockwise.
6. Bring the foot back, keeping the knee high.
7. Do the side kick, pivoting your left foot on the ball, another 90° anticlockwise (it's now heel-forward).

8. Place the foot down in front of you, in guard.
9. Repeat on the other side.

Kicking Targets

When it's comfortable to do all three together and you can do them at waist height without it feeling like a stretch, you are ready to start kicking things. To start with you will probably not be able to kick hard at all, and it may feel like the pad is pushing you back rather than the reverse. Remember, the key to power is relaxed, supported movement, so don't try to batter down the wall.

For this we use the kickpad, held in front for the front kick and side kick, and held against the thigh for the round kick (higher only if your partner is totally comfortable kicking higher).

When holding the pad, you also have to be relaxed and supported. Your objective is not to remain immobile, but to learn to absorb increasing amounts of force.

Other Exercises

Most people don't think of their feet as tools or weapons. To be a good kicker, that has to change. So there are lots of things you could do with your feet that you would normally do with your hands. I routinely turn lights on and off with my foot, open and close doors with them, and every now and then I do things like my dagger defences with my feet. Yes, you can parry a dagger strike with your foot. I don't recommend it as a first line of defence, nor do I think I could realistically defend myself against a dagger attack using only my feet (unless I ran away), but it's useful for getting your feet properly attached to your brain. *Play* with this, and soon enough your feet will do what you tell them.

You can also incorporate kicks into all your basic footwork drills. You should be able to kick with either foot in any guard position.

More Advanced Kicking

If you like kicking and want to go further than the above material, by all means do so. My next step is usually to add a reciprocal kick to each of the three, done in the opposite direction: front kick/back kick, round kick/hook kick and side kick/stomp.

1. Start on guard and do the front kick with your right foot.
2. As you bring your foot back, look over your right shoulder and kick straight back with your heel.
3. Bring the knee up and forwards, and do the round kick.
4. Sweep your foot back, leaving your knee and hips where they are, and hook across (left to right) with your heel.
5. Bring your foot back and do the side kick.
6. As you return your foot, keep your knee up and leave your supporting foot where it is. Look to your left (so, behind you) and do a low stomping kick in that direction.
7. Place the foot on the ground, where it would be if you had just passed forward instead of doing all those kicks, and repeat on the other leg.

Note that I have just introduced three new kicks (back, hook and stomp) without any preparation or introduction. This is the advanced book. I think you ought to be able to have a go at them; break out the ones that are hard into basic, single-kick drills; get them solid; and put them back into the six-kick drill – all without too much trouble and, most importantly, without injuring yourself. Carry on!

The back kick: Guy stands on guard, raises his foot (not the knee), and kicks.

The hook kick: Jan raises his knee, turns his supporting
foot and hip, and whips his heel across.

The stomp: Guy stomps with the instep against an imaginary shin.

Shortly after this draft was written and the photoshoot was over, we added crescent kicks, inside and outside, to the drill. I cannot emphasise enough how much training ideas and matters of interpretation and execution can change over time. Producing a second edition of a book takes months of work, but I can video, edit and upload additions and changes to our syllabus wiki in a matter of a few hours. So please do make use of it!

WITHDRAW UNDER COVER

This is done like part one of the *Farfalla di Ferro*, just passing backward instead of forward. It goes as follows.

1. You have just completed the high thrust towards the end of step sixteen and are continuing to the next step.
2. *Mandritto fendente* with a pass back.
3. Cut through to *fenestra sinestra*, thrust.
4. *Roverso fendente* with a pass back.
5. Cut through to *fenestra destra*.
6. Bring your feet together and your sword to rest upright on your left shoulder, ready to start the Form again.

Petteri has made the high thrust, passes backward with a *mandritto fendente*
and through *posta di dente di zenghiaro*; he keeps the sword in motion
towards *fenestra*, thrusts forward with *fenestra*, turns the sword around the
middle of the blade and strikes a *roverso fendente*. He passes backward
through *coda longa*, keeping the sword moving up towards *fenestra*, and
arrives in *fenestra* with a *volta stabile*.

The point of this is to train into you the idea that you keep moving
and you keep your guard up, until the fight is over and you are
out of measure again. There is no substitute for continual awareness.

I am a kind and patient man, most of the time. But the one habit
that drives me nuts is the tendency for my students, and everyone
else, to make the last strike of a drill and then think it's over *while
they are still in measure.* When that happens, and I am present, I
hit the student (not hard, and not vindictively) to get the message
across that if you collapse when within your opponent's reach, you
will, should, must and *deserve* to get hit. This is the foulest legacy
of using blunt swords and safety equipment, and of training safely
with nice people. It ruins your sense of danger.

By far the best martial artists in this regard tend to be those
doing Japanese budo or koryu. I have watched their practise and
done some myself (though not the sword arts). It goes like this:
the practitioners stand out of measure; bow to their opponents
(standing or kneeling); get into measure and do the drill; back away
under cover, carefully; and bow again when out of measure. The
basic drill therefore always includes getting into and out of measure
carefully, mindfully and attentively. And it is glorious to see done
well.

This last step of the Form is all about that. The fight ain't over until you are home safe. The key skill is focus. And nothing generates focus quite like sharp swords ...

PART THREE

TRAINING WITH SHARPS

In 2004 I was in America attending an instructors' retreat, and I was amazed to find practically everyone using aluminium wasters instead of steel. It made no sense to me then, and still makes none now. I was so astonished that I started a thread on SFI entitled "Aluminium wasters: NO!" It started something of a storm, with almost everyone wading in in defence of using simulators that are further removed from the real thing than necessary. On repeated visits to the USA I have watched the situation change, and at the last event I attended there was, I think, one aluminium longsword – out of about 150 participants – and everyone else was using steel. It was a major step in the right direction.

By this time, of course (and indeed for about six years prior) I had come around to the idea that, actually, blunt steel is already too much of a compromise, and that people can and should practise their skills with the real thing – a sharp sword. There is no question that sharp swords are what Fiore had in mind, and anyone who has executed the plays sharp-on-sharp can tell you that the weapons behave very differently to even blunt steel and are quite unlike any other simulator. So I think that, once the basic mechanics are working for you and the likelihood of slicing off your own ear has diminished, practising solo drills with a sharp sword is the next logical step; then test cutting, and then sharp-on-sharp drills with a partner. I liken this to practising pistol shooting. No one I've ever met seriously suggests that you should do combat training scenarios by shooting live rounds at each other: paint bullets make much more sense. But, equally, no one seriously suggests that you can learn to shoot without ever using live ammunition. It is significantly easier to kill or maim someone with a loaded gun than with a sharp sword, so if we treat our sharps with the same respect with which we would treat a firearm, then accidents will be acceptably rare.

So, the first step is to acquire a sharp steel sword and go through all your solo drills with it. In practice this is no different to using a blunt, but the stakes are higher – you really can take an ear off if your *posta di donna* is wrong.

Test Cutting

(The section on test cutting is adapted, with permission, from my article in *Western Martial Arts Illustrated*, issue 2, fall 2007.)

Cutting objects with a sharp sword is a vital research and training method for practitioners of historical (or any other kind of) swordsmanship. It is usually referred to as "test cutting" because in the traditional Japanese sword arts new swords would be tested by an expert swordsman, who would cut through prisoners or soaked rice-straw targets, and then grade the sword accordingly (a process known as *tameshigiri*). The soaked straw was chosen because it apparently closely simulated the muscle and connective tissue in the human body. There are, in fact, three subjects to be tested with cutting practice. Those are:

1. the cut itself: how changes in cutting style can alter the effectiveness of the cut;
2. the sword: how changes in sharpness, blade geometry or length affect the cut; and
3. the substrate: how well different materials stand up to a sword.

In any single cutting session it is very important to limit the above variables to one. For example, if you wish to examine different cutting styles, use the same sword and the same targets so that you know for sure what is causing the changes.

It is almost impossible to simulate a combat situation when doing cutting practice: opponents do not stand still. Neither is it easy to exactly simulate a human body in the normal fencing protection of the style in question. The best simulation from that perspective is almost certainly (given that we can't use people) to cover a large bit of dead pig with a gambeson and/or mail or plate, take an accurately reconstructed period sword and see what kind of damage occurs when striking the pig with various types of blow. Unfortunately, there are no metallurgically accurate reproductions on the market that I know of. Even the cheapest modern longsword is usually made of far better steel than that which would have been available in the period. So, already, our research is hampered by having too good a sword.

However, we do know that swords of this period could cut very effectively. Perhaps the most famous example comes from the Chronicle of Pero Niño, started in 1431 and concluded sometime after 1449. In it, the chronicler Gutierre Diaz de Gamez records that in 1396 Pero Niño was aboard King Enrique II of Spain's galley and was being rowed up the Guadalquivir river to Seville. Some fishermen, unaware of the King's progress, had strung a hawser "as thick as a man's knee" across the river, supporting a net for catching shad. The rope would have swept the galley deck and overturned the vessel had our hero not "leapt briskly to the prow, drew his sword and gave it such a blow that he broke the hawser … wherefore all were amazed". This feat argues for two things: those are a good sword and an excellent swordsman – one who has probably practised cutting targets a fair bit. The skeletons dug up from medieval battlefields (of which Wisby is perhaps the best known example) also show horrific instances of the damage done by swords against the human body.

The question for us researchers is this: how do we simulate the target, and how do we assess the effect of the cutting actions we learn from the treatises?

When designing the target we need to take the following things into account.

- Verisimilitude: how well does it simulate the "real" target?
- Cost: how much money and time does it take to prepare?
- Consistency: how similar can we make each target piece, to ensure minimum variations that might affect the resistance to cutting?
- Damage: will the target materials damage the sword and, if so, is that acceptable? Blood and water rust steel, bones can chip blades, straw scratches, etc.

The following targets seem popular in current WMA circles: Japanese-style mats made from soft rush material (*tatami omote*);

beach mats (used the same way as *tatami* – they're cheaper but do more damage to the sword and are less consistent); animal parts; cardboard tubes; carpet rolls; dangling rope; plastic bottles filled with water; rolls of newspaper; and newspaper rolled around a plastic tube to simulate bone (this last comes from David Lindholm's *Knightly Art of the Longsword*, page 225). Paper products such as newsprint or cardboard can carry the abrasive grit used in the pulping process, which will scratch and may dull your sword. Given the range available, it makes sense to try out the ones suitable for your training environment. In each case the targets vary according to their weight, density, hardness, how much resistance the materials give to the blade (mats, rope and paper are usually soaked to lubricate the cut and soften the fibres; this also more closely simulates the conditions in the human body), and how stable the target is on impact. A dangling rope is much harder to cut than one held taut because it can move away from the cut. Likewise, the same rope is easier to cut with a downwards blow than a rising one. An empty plastic bottle standing on a level surface is harder to cut than the same bottle filled with water, because the weight of the water holds the bottle in place at the moment of impact. It is necessary that the target be cut-able by the sword in question: no sword should be used to cut down a tree (that's why loggers used axes). Where armour is placed over the target (such as putting a gambeson sleeve over a leg of pork), it is important to be clear whether it is the armour, the sword or the cut being tested. I have found that the *tatami omote*, though laborious to prepare and relatively expensive to obtain, are the most consistent and hence most useful cutting substrate.

The sharpness of the sword is also an issue. People who specialise in test cutting tend to prefer a very sharp edge, because it cuts better. However, practising technical drills with sharp swords teaches you first and foremost that during a sword fight a very sharp edge gets damaged worse and faster than a slightly dull one, and that any sword that can be considered sharp will incur damage to the edge on contact with another sword. Medieval combat styles often include half-sword technique, whereby the sword is grasped by handle and blade: a super-sharp edge makes this risky, but an ordinarily sharp sword will not cut the hand unless the blade is drawn across it. For cutting practice it is perfectly acceptable to use an over-sharp sword, provided that we take into account the excessive sharpness when estimating the blow's effectiveness in combat.

It is not actually necessary to simulate a body part at all for the purposes of testing the effect of different styles of cut or testing changes to your cutting technique: any consistent target that is appropriate for cutting will do to start with. Careful examination of the target and the blow should tell you whether your cut is hitting (but not cutting) or whether it's slicing through easily, how accurate the blow was, what part of the edge cuts best, how your footwork (if any) affects the blow, and how much effort the effect is costing you. Video taping the cutting session is extremely useful for those purposes, as is the presence of a competent instructor.

The cut is affected by the following factors.

1. The sword
   - sharpness;
   - blade geometry (edge straight or curved, edge profile and distribution of mass);
   - steel used (primarily affects how quickly the blade gets blunt, but also laminations cause micro-serrations on the edge, which make slicing more effective); and
   - blade harmonics (how the blade vibrates when swung and on impact).

2. The target
   - resistance of the material, and
   - stability.

3. The mechanics of the cut, in
   - blade speed and mass (faster blades cut better, and heavier ones are more stable);
   - blade alignment (the edge angle must be in line with the swing angle; different cutting angles have different effects); and
   - blade stability (how well the blade is supported by the cutter and how much the blade vibrates on impact).

The biggest problem faced by most practitioners of swordsmanship when doing sharp cutting practise is the lack of tactical feedback from the target. It is an unfortunate fact of swordsmanship life that the most effective cut on a static target is usually wildly untactical but incredibly satisfying to do. We feel rewarded when the sword hisses through the target with no apparent effort, and so we naturally change our cutting style to make it happen. This often leads to cuts that are initiated in the hips, with the sword trailing. Done in combat, this is clearly one of Silver's false times. By exposing ourselves to a counterattack, our lovely, powerful cut never actually lands, because we stop the opponent's sword with our face first. Setting up a video camera behind the target allows us to examine this; also, a competent instructor will spot it and tell you to stop.

It is important at this point to understand that test cutting is only one part of a swordsman's training. Since we are training with edged weapons it is important to make sure that we know how to make the best use of that edge in the context of our Art. Test cutting is common to most swordsmanship styles worldwide. So it affords an excellent opportunity for cross-training with martial artists from other disciplines, and also provides a chance to dispel myths about our weapons and styles.

So, for research purposes, we can idealise the sword (making it unreasonably sharp), idealise the target (making it stand still), and then vary the mechanics of the cut to see what hits hard and what cuts. The two are not the same, and it is as well to remember that being hit hard on the head by a long piece of steel is always going to have some effect. Whether you completely sever his head or just slice halfway through his neck is unlikely to make much difference in combat. There are many different ways to cut correctly, and there are many different purposes for cutting. It is perfectly reasonable to conclude that a cut of type A is excellent for slicing soft tissue, type B works best for bashing skulls and type C is only any use for stationary cutting (for example, for testing blade sharpness or the effect of different blade profiles).

In any case, cutting practice is vital for historical swordsmanship practitioners, and it can yield important feedback about the swords in question or a given cutting style. There is a world of difference though between unscientific "let's have a go at cutting stuff" practice and properly thought-out cutting research and training. And, above all, cutters should remember that targets don't avoid, parry or hit back.

Sharp on Sharp

If you have no doubt about your competence to train safely with sharps, go away and train harder for a few more years and come back with a decent sense of humility and respect for the thousands and thousands of people who have died by the sword over the millennia. This Art requires the most serious attention and awareness. A little self-doubt breeds respect. Respect breeds safety. Pair training with sharps is obviously dangerous, so be very careful.

That said, with a sharp sword that you don't mind getting banged up and a partner you have trained with extensively and trust implicitly, put on your full freeplay equipment and go **slowly and carefully** through the basic drills. Pay especial attention to actions that involve extended blade contact, such as the breaking of the thrust and the binds. It usually only takes one iteration of the breaking of the thrust to convert sceptics to the usefulness of sharp-on-sharp training. Sharp blades stick, so larger binding actions are much easier and so make more sense. Sharp blades are so much more responsive and feed so much more information into the hand.

My pair-drill sharp is banged up from *tutta* through the *mezza*, but the *punta di spada* is almost unscathed. Given that this is the bit you hit with, it can and should be as sharp as you like, because it won't take much damage anyway.

Perhaps the most dangerous aspect of sharp-on-sharp training is that going back to blunt steel feels like a much safer and more comfortable environment – so respect diminishes and risk increases. A blunt steel sword can kill. A sharp sword just does it with less effort.

Sharp Swords

Sharpness is relative. A sword that is more than sharp enough to go through a man with a thrust, or cut his head completely off, may not be sharp enough for really successful cutting practice on targets such as a hanging rope or *tatami omote* (rush mats soaked and rolled, a traditional Japanese cutting target). In practice, the edge should be just sharp enough for its intended purpose: the sharper the edge, the more fragile it becomes. So a fighting sword will not normally be honed to a razor edge, but one for test cutting will be. Likewise, pair drills done sharp-to-sharp do quite a bit of damage to the sword, and I can't afford to be spending several thousand euros every few years for a new one. (Yes, I do advocate practising with sharp swords and in carefully controlled conditions.) For this reason, I use three longswords in normal practice: a blunt and two sharps. The sharps are a hand-made poem in steel by J.T. Pälikkö for solo work and test cutting, and an off-the-shelf, good quality but much cheaper weapon by Angus Trim for pair work.

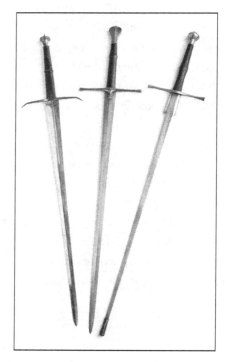

Sharpness and Sharpening

The perfect edge is two mirror-polished bevels meeting at an acute angle. The exact angle will depend on the desired result, and the blunt sword should of course have a rounded edge.

The more acute the angle, the less resistance the target will give; but the less metal there is supporting the edge, so the more fragile it becomes. The objective of sharpness is to minimise the surface area of the edge that makes contact with the target. This is achieved by making the edge as close to a single molecule of steel as is practicable. Any scratches in the facets of the edges increase the length of the edge by creating a micro-serration or miniature nick.

Sharpening is the process of creating those facets at the correct angle and of the correct polish by removing as much steel as necessary but no more. These days, the best tools for that job, especially for non-specialists, are a set of diamond laps with an edge angle guide.

I would not recommend you to begin your sharpening practice on your shiny new sword. Get very good at sharpening knives (you'll find some in the kitchen) before trying to sharpen a sword. The length of the blade and its cross-section (usually diamond) makes it much more difficult to keep the sharpening angle consistent. I spent five years as a furniture maker, sharpening chisels and knives almost every day, and I have been sharpening knives and other tools for over thirty years, and yet I still prefer to get a specialist to put an edge on my swords.

A sharp steel sword is necessary if you want to do cutting practice and actually cut things up. It is also very useful when doing solo practice, and advanced students should be able to perform all drills slowly with sharps.

The Cutter

This sword should be over-sharp – sharper than you would expect on a combat weapon. A thin, wide blade will tend to cut objects better than a thick but narrow one, because it passes through the target without getting wedged. But any sharp sword will cut if swung right.

The Pair Drill Sharp

Anyone conducting serious research, and certainly anyone who considers themselves a professional in this field, should test each and every action with sharp steel, not least because the techniques are designed to work sharp-against-sharp, and sharp swords behave differently to blunt ones. With proper protection and a high degree of control, there is far less danger using sharps than there is when under-trained students freeplay with each other. Every single advanced student at my school has done our core drills with sharps, and every single technique in this book has been repeatedly tested with sharps. This will seriously mash up your sword. I have had my current sharp re-ground about three times in the last five years and, while the tip area is still quite undamaged, the rest of the blade is nicked and notched. This sword need not be sharp enough to effortlessly slice through *tatami*, but it should be sharp enough to cut a cabbage in half. You can see the edge damage in this photo:

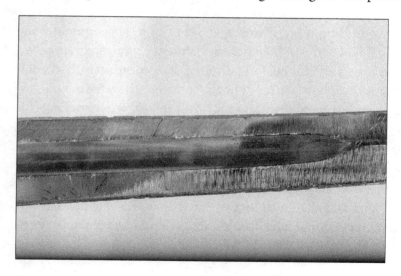

Edge damage from pair work with sharps.

So, in practise, I use three types of longsword: a blunt trainer, a beautiful, custom-made sharp for test-cutting and a much cheaper sharp sword for pair work.

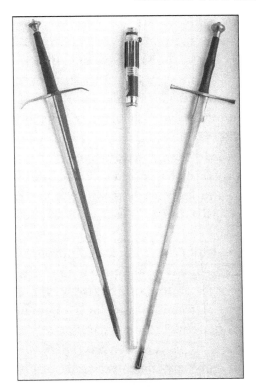

The Pälikkö cuts like a lightsaber.

Why you should train with sharp swords, and how to go about it without killing anyone

The following article was originally a guest post on the *Chivalric Fighting Arts Association* blog, and I wrote it to help serious students of swordsmanship arts get over the problem of how to incorporate sharp swords into their training. It was published there on 18 February 2014.

Swords are, by definition, sharp. Anything sword-like that is not sharp is either a foil or a percussive weapon like a club. I am a swordsman, and so I use sharp swords. Do I let my beginner students fight each other (or even handle) sharps? No, of course not. But my senior students have done all the basic drills in our longsword syllabus sharp-on-sharp.

I would go so far as to say that if you haven't done it with sharps, you haven't done it at all. The arts that I practise were all intended for combat with sharp swords. There are two main differences between training with blunts and training with sharps: the way the weapons behave on contact, and the psychological factor. Sharp swords tend to stick together when they meet; blunt swords slide off each other. This makes binds, winds, transports and other blade-on-blade actions more difficult with blunts. Also, there is nothing that demands your attention quite like a sharp sword pointed at your face. You behave differently when the swords are sharp: you're more attentive, more alert, more focussed and more careful. More alive. The conservative tactical choices that the treatises tend to favour make much more sense.

It is well to remember that you are compromising your swordsmanship when you practise safely and are not attempting to harm your partner. So we do lots of practise with blunts and sharps, at every degree of freedom and level of intent. (I've written extensively on this concept on page 232-256 of *Swordfighting, for writers, game designers, and martial artists.*) Sharpening the sword does not eliminate the compromise, it just moves it from the tool to the level of intent. Blunt swords and wooden wasters have their place in swordsmanship training, and they always have done. With sharps you can practise full-intent actions alone or against inanimate targets; and careful actions, up to and including light freeplay, with a partner. You can do all of that with blunts too, and also more vigorous actions such as full-speed freeplay. It is also possible to use a sword-simulator that is sharp in the middle of the blade and blunted at the tip, which gives you most of the binding and handling characteristics of a true sharp with much less risk, and so fewer of the psychological characteristics. This can form a bridge between blunt-only and full-sharp training, and can also allow you to freeplay with a tool that binds properly.

The question "should we train with sharps" simply does not arise in many other blade-oriented martial arts. In Escrima, for instance, drills are usually done with sticks or sharps. On every one of Kaj Westersund's knife courses I've attended, we have done drills with sharps; only on some of them did we use blunt training knives at all. In a ten-weekend seminar series there was, I think, one minor cut that was not self-inflicted. (The balisong weekend was a blood-bath! Thirteen self-inflicted minor cuts in the first hour. It was hilarious.) Traditional Japanese sword arts are similar. If you read Dave Lowry's *Autumn Lightning*, a memoir of his childhood spent mostly training martial arts, you find that after many months of using a bokken (a wooden sword) he, while still in high school, started using a sharp:

> "But unleashing a yard-long, wickedly sharp sword out of a scabbard inches from my belly, slashing with it, and then sliding it back into its sheath, again only a finger's distance from my abdomen, was one of the most frightening things I had ever done. It was worse by far than the time my best friend and I went canoeing on a flooded river and nearly drowned... It was the only distraction that could occupy more of my attention than Linda Smith's legs, stretched out two rows in front of me. Teachers who saw me walking to classes with a fretful look about me probably concluded I was worried about acne, or a relationship with a girl like Linda Smith. It's a safe bet they never suspected I was really wondering how many stitches it would take to close the gash opened by a carelessly handled samurai katana." (P. 106.)

Sure, it's frightening. It should be. But isn't swordsmanship all about behaving well in scary situations?

Our treatises from before the 1500s don't seem to address the issue. As far as I know, the earliest reference is in the introduction to Book Six of Manciolino's *Opera Nova* (1531), which begins as follows:

> "I now wish to show how wrong those are who insist that good swordsmanship can never proceed from practice with blunted weapons, but only from training with sharp swords. ... It is far preferable to learn to strike with bated blades then with sharp ones; and it would not be fair to arm untrained students with sharp swords or with other weapons that can inflict injury for the purpose of training new students to defend themselves."

I couldn't agree more. I start all my students with blunt steel swords, and I introduce sharps when they are ready for them.

So the questions are: when, how and how much?

1. "When should sharps be incorporated in a student's training?"

When students are thoroughly able to control a longsword simulator and have a solid grounding in basic technique, they should start incorporating work with sharps as soon as possible. In my school we have a set basic syllabus, which allows us to track student progress quite precisely. I would say that once the student has passed our four basic levels she should, while she begins to add freeplay into her practise, also go back to the beginning and do it all again with sharps; at first she should only do this with me, and then under the guidance of an experienced senior.[1]

2. "How do I incorporate sharps safely?"

Incorporating sharps in training is totally dependent on local conditions. It is unworkable for some and straightforward for others. Local experience levels and local legal conditions vary wildly. Just bear in mind that all physical activities have injury rates, and an accident does not necessarily kill the club. Obviously, my solutions are adapted for a formal school. Other groups may not be able to implement them, but I suggest talking to other martial arts clubs in your area that do use sharps (there are bound to be some) before dismissing the possibility as an insurance nightmare.

Normally in my classes, a student's first time handling a sharp sword happens when I take a person individually, put a sword in her hand and take her through a basic pair drill. This is not reproducible, though, so here are other options for instructors. Let us assume that whoever is leading the class has sufficient experience with sharps to do this.

- Cutting seminars; let everyone have a go. There is no real risk at all when these are run properly, and students learn much

---

1 My use of "she" here caused some speculation about political correctness and other such tomfoolery. At the time of writing the last student I had done this exercise with was female, and so she was the person in my head when I was writing this up. Make of this what you will.

about how sharps work. In this context you can even take people who have never handled any kind of sword before and get them to safely cut a *tatami* mat, or similar. I've done this in public demonstrations with members of the audience.

- In our syllabus we introduce doing drills with sharps at level five. This is after the student has completed the basic levels and is beginning freeplay, too. Usually in their first advanced class (which are scheduled separately: beginners can watch but not train), I take them one at a time through a couple of basic drills that they know really well. No protection for the student. I may wear a mask if they are really worried. (Almost every student I've done this with was more worried about injuring than getting injured.) You can do this in protective kit if you want, but that tends to generate a false sense of security.
- At this level of their training I also encourage my students to do all solo training with a sharp, if they can buy or borrow one.
- Once they are habituated they can do any drill with sharps at any time. My senior students are always working on a specific training issue. If their issue is best addressed with sharps then that's the tool they will choose.

It is more difficult with thrust-oriented weapons like rapier and smallsword because thrusts to the face or body are much harder to control than cuts, and they are more likely to cause permanent damage. I think all students of any system should practise test-cutting and test-thrusting, and I normally demonstrate rapier drills with the person "winning" that step of the drill holding a blunt, and the person getting hit holding a sharp. That way you are really careful to get the opponent's sword out of the way before lunging forwards. And exercises like "Hunt the Debole", which do not involve striking, can easily and usefully be done with sharps. So it takes a bit of thinking about, but it can be done.

3. "How much training should be done with sharps?"

Angelo Viggiani (in *Lo Schermo*, 1575, page 52v-53r) was insistent that all training be done with sharps. Note, though, that his student in the book is already an experienced swordsman. This is one of my favourite passages in all of swordsmanship literature, so much so that I'll repeat it again here. ROD is Rodomonte, Viggiani's character in the book; CON is Conte, the Count that Rodomonte is giving a lesson to.

"ROD: ... take up your sword, Conte.

CON: How so, my sword? Isn't it better to take one meant for practice?

ROD: Not now, because with those practice weapons it is not possible to acquire valor or prowess of the heart, nor ever to learn a perfect *schermo*.

CON: I believe the former, but the latter I doubt. What is the reason, Rodomonte, that it is not possible to learn (so you say) a perfect *schermo* with that sort of weapon? Can't you deliver the same blows with that, as with one which is edged?

ROD: I would not say now that you cannot do all those ways of striking, of warding, and of guards, with those weapons, and equally with these, but you will do them imperfectly with those, and most perfectly with these edged ones, because if (for example) you ward a thrust put to you by the enemy, beating aside his sword with a *mandritto*, so that that thrust did not face your breast, while playing with *spade da marra*, it will suffice you to beat it only a little, indeed, for you to learn the *schermo*; but if they were *spade da filo*, you would drive that *mandritto* with all of your strength in order to push well aside the enemy's thrust. Behold that this would be a perfect blow, done with wisdom, and with promptness, unleashed with more length, and thrown with more force, than it would have been with those other arms. How will you fare, Conte, if you take perfect arms in your hand, and not stand with all your spirit, and with all your intent judgment?

CON: Yes, but it is a great danger to train with arms that puncture; if I were to make the slightest mistake, I could do enormous harm. Nonetheless we will indeed do as is more pleasing to you, because you will be on guard not to harm me, and I will be certain to parry, and I will pay constant attention to your point in order to know which blow may come forth from your hand, which is necessary in a good warrior."

While I adore this book, I don't think that all training should be done with sharps, even for experienced swordsmen. Competitive sparring, for instance, is best done using a tool you feel able to really strike with. But in my ideal world all solo drills and set drills would be done with sharps, once a certain level of competence has been reached. You may note that, in the excerpt above, Viggiani is teaching an experienced swordsman a set drill.

If you are thinking to yourself "this is all very well, but I am not experienced enough to do pair drills with sharps yet", then firstly, you're probably right; secondly, you may instead be ready to do the solo drills and test-cutting with sharps. You may also want to go to a professional to train you past this hurdle. I routinely do unprotected sharps drills with students I don't know at seminars. WMAW 2011 is a good example. There, I offered the class the opportunity to do some basic drill (often the breaking of the thrust, which is much easier to do with sharps than with blunts, and a variant on the Four Crossings drill) sharp-on sharp- with me, with no masks or other protection. All of the forty-or-so students took me up on it (I was expecting about ten). Many of them came up to me afterwards and said it was one of the most important training experiences of their lives. This encouraged me to risk losing my sharps at Customs when I went to Melbourne in 2013; they have very strict sword laws in the state of Victoria. (I declared them, and there was no problem getting them through with the right paperwork.) It was worth the risk. On that trip, almost everyone at the seminar got to experience pair work with sharps; again, it opened their eyes and minds to an amazing degree. As Shannon Walker wrote in his review of that seminar:

> *"Guy Windsor is known for saying: 'if you haven't trained with a sharp sword, you haven't trained to fight with a sword at all.'*
> *Like others in the HEMA community, I always took that with a grain of salt. After all, I've been training with the Melbourne Swordplay Guild and the Glen Lachlann Estate College of Arms in Melbourne for over four years, using blunt weapons, and I think I have a reasonable grasp of what it would be like with actual swords.*

And then Guy stood in Posta Longa in front of me with a sharp longsword to explain a technique and I realised, quite simply, I was wrong. Sharps make a world of difference. There was no way – NO WAY – I was going to attempt techniques against a sharp I would normally have been happy to try against a blunt."

Most frightening was a demonstration I did last summer at Ropecon, a major roleplaying convention here in Helsinki. The theme of the demonstration was sharps vs. blunts and I allowed members of the audience, whom I did not know, to have a go. This is wildly different to doing it in a seminar, where I've had an hour or more to assess and prepare the students beforehand.

The way I set it up was really important. It came at the end of the demo, and so they were habituated to listening to me. They did a slow drill, using blunts and wearing masks, with a senior student so that they would get some experience with a longsword first, and would get used to following directions. Also, it was a filter for undesirables (there were none).

The set-up had the attendees with their backs to the audience, and I had five students in uniform and the senior assistant behind me. Literally, they had my back. So those having a go were clearly in MY space. They were each handed a sword in turn by another assistant. They were primed, psychologically, to follow directions before we faced each other with sharps.

Most of them had some background in weapons martial arts, but not all of them. Everybody (especially me) learned something. And nobody got hurt.

I did this for three reasons.

1. It was a really useful experience for most of the participants, especially the martial artists, and it was memorable for all.
2. It clearly differentiated what we do from the Boffer Tournament and other events.
3. It was a useful training experience for me. I was utterly focussed on the person I was training with, while keeping half an eye on the crowd. It was an exercise in awareness and control.

In my experience about one in three students do something suicidal while facing a sharp so, really, it's me keeping us both alive. That's okay. And if I fail one day, that's okay too. I think the risk is worth it. It is an unparalleled learning experience, and is simply essential when working on an interpretation. If you haven't tested it with sharps, you haven't tested it at all. I would not tell a class outside of my school "now go do this with sharps" the way I will with my senior students. But as a service to the students present, I accept the risks of sharp-on-sharp with people I don't know. I just prepare them – one way or another – really carefully beforehand, create a safe environment and make the assumption that they will try to stab me and try to run onto my point, before we cross swords. This is my job. I would not expect any amateur to take that kind of risk; the cost-benefit analysis would not work out.

A decade of injury-free sharps training suggests that even without masks the risks aren't that high, because they are so obvious: more obvious than the risks when driving. In fact, almost all the training injuries I've seen happened during freeplay with blunts. This is because of the human tendency to apply risk home-ostasis: you are intuitively comfortable with a certain level of perceived risk, and you will take more risks in what you think is a safer environment. Ironically, based on our injury record, I would say that training with sharps is safer than training with blunts!

I hope that this article demonstrates that training with sharps is a necessary and achievable aspect of learning the Art of swords-manship. Let me finish on this note though: if you feel totally competent and comfortable to train with sharp swords, that is a good indication that you are either a master swordsman way beyond my level, or that you are dangerously deluded. Much of the value of the sharps comes from the clear and present danger they embody. Please make sure that you can see it and feel it before you draw your sword from its scabbard.

USING THE FORM

O nce you have the Form in memory, you can use it for all sorts of other things. One of my favourites is practising at multiple speeds.

- Treacle speed: go so slowly that every step is an exercise in hovering. This is really, really hard. Good. It will smooth you out.
- Walking speed: this is the normal speed at which you will stroll through the Form, not rushing, but not too slow: a nice, comfortable pace. Like this, I get through the whole Form in about 45 seconds.
- Fast: this is where it all goes to shit. Go as fast as you can. This should hurt – hurt not least your pride and your sense of aesthetics, when actions that were quite accurate suddenly get really sloppy.
- Continuously: put on some music (I usually use *the Eye of the Tiger* for this), start your Form when the music starts, and do not stop for any reason (except to prevent injury) until the music stops. Every action in the Form begins and ends in one guard or another. So whenever you find yourself in, for example, *posta di fenestra destra*, you can do whatever actions fit the Form from there. You could just repeat the Form over and over, but I like to play with it.

Learning to Attack

Alert readers will have noticed that there is only one successful attack in the Form. The rest of the steps are all defences. This balance of 1/17 is not far off the pattern shown in the Getty manuscript. Between the defence of the sword in the scabbard through to the end of the sword in armour, there are (depending on how you count them, but approximately) 75 plays. Of these, a total of four are counter-remedies: the counter to the *punta falsa*, two counters to the *ligadura mezana* and the elbow push done with the sword in armour.

This does not mean that attacks are doomed to fail, but it seems reasonable that our core treatise memory palace should have a similar structure. However, attacking successfully is a hugely important skill, and one which the Form embodies in step four. In essence, the defence is either a parry or a counterattack. If it's a parry, you can either beat the parry through speed, deceive it with a feint or counter the riposte. If it is a (properly done) counterattack, you must parry. Knowing this, you can now work through the applications to the Form step by step and add a counter-remedy to each remedy. This should be very straightforward.

- Steps 2, 10 and 17 are not defences per se, and so do not necessarily have counters. There is room, though, for you to use your imagination. Alternatively, just recall the applications to the *Farfalla di Ferro* (step 2).
- Steps 11 (the *punta falsa*) and 12 (the sword in armour) have canonical counter-remedies in the treatise; and if you look at step 8 and notice it includes a *ligadura mezana*, you should have no trouble applying the counter-remedies to it as shown in the fifteenth and sixteenth plays of the *zogho stretto*.
- Steps 5, 6, 7, 9 and 14 are all embedded in the basic syllabus as part of set drills that have set counters, so that should be no problem.
- This leaves only steps 1, 3, 13, 15 and 16 for you to work out from scratch. I would suggest that this is not a difficult exercise, given the vast store of examples you could follow.

The obvious *lacuna* now is how to attack against a point in line guard. As Fiore says, on f24r:

"E zaschuna altra guardia in larte una simile de laltra sie contrario salvo le guardie che stano in punta, zoe posta lunga e breve e meza porta di ferro che punta per punta la piu lunga fa offesa inanci."

Translation:

> "And every other guard in the art, one like another is the counter; except the guards that stand in the point, so *posta longa*, and *breve*, and *meza porta di ferro*, that point for point, the longer makes offence first."

I read this to mean that you can counter any of your opponent's guards with the same guard (which makes sense: if you are equal, you are not disadvantaged), except for the guards that have the point in line; in that case, the person with the longer reach (be that a longer sword, longer arms or both) could strike first.

So, how should you approach the point in line guards? You basically have three options.

1. Beat the sword out of the way if it is extended (*longa* or *bicorno*).
2. Attack to draw the prepared thrust, and then counter it.
3. Attack to force a parry, and then counter it.

Of course, your opponent has their own ideas, and they may know this book as well as you do. If you go to beat their sword out of the way, they could avoid it (like avoiding a parry), or they may allow it and counter your actual attack; if you attack to draw their prepared thrust, they could deceive you again by, for instance, not accepting your invitation, or by accepting it in an unexpected line; if you attack to draw their parry, they may sneak in a counterattack, or they could parry and strike in a way that prevents your counter-remedy; and so on.

So what should you do? Work on this with tricky opponents, using the rule of Cs in reverse. Start with competition, see what works and what fails; then work backwards to coaching, where whoever was winning repeats their actions so that their partner can learn to counter them; and from this derive set drills to crystallise what you have learned into a memorable form.

Did I just say "form"?

The Syllabus Form Applications Drill

This drill is a great way to see how well a group of students really knows the Form. You start off with one person in the middle and doing the Form, which is timed. For any time under 50 seconds, add five.

Let's say Sanniina does the Form in 45 seconds on her own. We add five, to make 50 seconds.

Then two or three assistants have to give her the correct stimulus from the correct direction and in the correct measure to create all the basic set applications of the Form in order. Sanniina just walks through her Form. Ilpo, Henry and Satu scurry about to be in the correct place at the correct time; Ilpo with the dagger, perhaps; Henry behind him, ready to thrust from *fenestra* after Sanniina has done the *Farfalla di Ferro*; Satu off to the correct side and in the correct guard, ready to receive Sanniina's feint; and so on.

For every second over the agreed 50, everyone does one push-up. This creates a certain social stress (don't make a mistake or my friends do push-ups) and a certain level of fatigue builds up. By the time all four students were done after one particularly disastrous round of this, they had each done over one hundred push-ups in addition to the Form, the scurrying around and so on.

Repeat the drill until everyone has been in the middle at least once.

I am sure you can come up with a hundred other ways to use and apply the Form. If you come up with something new, please do share it with me!

FINAL REMARKS

Advanced technique is basic technique done really well. Every cool trick or clever fight-winning secret technique is just a basic strike, lock or throw done in a more sophisticated context or in a more sophisticated way. There are no secrets. There are no magic tricks. But when your technique approaches excellence, those farther back along the path will think that you're a sorceror.

But you know perfectly well that you are not a sorceror. This is because as your skills improve, your ability to see flaws improves at the same time, and so you will remain deeply dissatisfied with your current level. Or, at least, you should, because there is always something to be working on – something that is not quite where it should be. How do you find it?

Run a diagnostic, identify the weakest link, create a strategy for strengthening that link, apply the strategy, and then test again using the same diagnostic. Do this over and over again, forever.

This sounds pretty bleak until you learn to take pride and pleasure in *how far you have come.*

I recommend videoing yourself doing drills, Form or freeplay (or all of the above), and then filing the video away for six months or a year. Then video yourself again, doing the same thing. While it might feel like you have not improved at all, it should be really obvious when you play the videos side by side which is the "before" and which is the "after". Enjoy that feeling of "I got better", and relish the feeling of "but there is so much left to improve". Then ruthlessly examine the newer video for every flaw and weakness and get back to work!

This way lies greatness, or so I believe. Check in with me in another decade or two and we'll see.

BIBLIOGRAPHY

F or an enormous bibliography of useful books and sources, please see *Swordfighting for Writers, Gamers and Martial Artists*. Here is a list of the sources mentioned in this book and further reading from the same author.

Primary Sources:

Il Fior di Battaglia (MS Ludwig XV13), J. P. Getty museum in Los Angeles.

Il Fior di battaglia di Fiore dei Liberi da Cividale (*Il Codice Ludwig XV 13 del* J. Paul Getty Museum), Massimo Malipiero, 2006.

Fiore de' Liberi's Fior di Battaglia, translation into English by Tom Leoni, 2009.

Flos Duellatorum, in private hands in Italy, but published in facsimile in 1902 by Francesco Novati.

Fior di Battaglia, Morgan MS M 383, Pierpont Morgan museum, New York.

Florius de Arte Luctandi (MSS LATIN 11269), Bibliotheque Nationale Francaise in Paris.

De Arte Gladiatoria Dimicandi, Filippo Vadi, Biblioteca Nazionale, Rome.

Gran Simulacro del arte e del uso della scherma, Ridolfo Capoferro, 1610.

Secondary Sources:

The Unconquered Knight: the Chronicle of Pero Niño, Gutierre Diaz de Gamez, tr. Joan Evans, 2004.

Knightly Art of the Longsword, David Lindholm, 2003.

Wolf Hall, Hilary Mantel, 2009 (epigram is from page 517).

"Unconscious cerebral initiative and the role of conscious will in voluntary action". Benjamin Libet, 1985. Published in The Behavioral and Brain Sciences 8: 529–566.

Further Reading

If you've enjoyed this book, you might like my blog (guywindsor. net/blog). Also, please consider buying one or more of the following:

The Swordsman's Quick Guide: a series of short booklets solving specific swordsmanship problems. So far the series includes: *The Seven Principles of Mastery, Choosing a Sword, Preparing for Freeplay, Ethics,* and *Teaching a Martial Arts Class.*

The Swordsman's Companion, a training manual for medieval longsword, 2004.

The Duellist's Companion, a training manual for seventeeth-century Italian rapier, 2006.

The Little Book of Push-ups, 2009. The title says it all.

The Armizare Vade Mecum, mnemonic verses for remembering Fiore's Art, 2011.

Mastering the Art of Arms vol. 1: The Medieval Dagger, a training manual for Fiore's dagger material, 2012.

Veni VADI Vici, a transcription and translation of Filippo Vadi's *De Arte Gladiatoria Dimicandi*, with commentary and analysis, 2012.

Mastering the Art of Arms vol. 2: The Medieval Longsword, a training manual for Fiore's longsword material, 2013.

Swordfighting, for Writers, Game Designers, and Martial Artists, 2015. Note especially the chapters on Talent and overcoming Barriers to Success.

If you already have them all, thank you for your generous support of my work!

Finally, let me ask you now to review this book, for better or worse, wherever is convenient for you. If I've done something right I need to know to do it again; moreover, I need to know what could be improved. As Vadi wrote:

"And if this my little work finds its way into the hands of anyone versed in the Art and appears to him to have anything superfluous or wrong, please adjust, reduce or add to it as he pleases. Because in the end I place myself under his correction and censure."

Thank you!

INDIEGOGO CAMPAIGN CONTRIBUTORS

Zoë Chandler
Zebee Johnstone
Yancy Orchard
Wendy Marques
Walter Neubauer
Voltemoy
Vittorio James Sgro
Ville Kankainen
Ville Henell
Tuomo Aimonen
Topi Mikkola
Tom and Aaron
   Karnuta
Toby Rodgers
Ting Hsu
Timo Kurvi
Tim Trant
Tim Makofske
Thomas Riley
Thomas Milbradt
Thomas Cole
Thomas Belloma
Tero Alanko
Teemu Kari
Tea Kew
Tapio Pellinen
Steve Planchin
Stephen Hobson
Stephen Cull
Sophie Marshall
Simone Zarbin
Sherratt Pemberton
Shayne Lynch
Shawn Weese
Shannon Walker
Shane Kennedy
Seth A Surber
Sean Mehonoshen
Scott Nimmo
Scott Aldinger

Schwertkampf
   Osnabrueck e.V.
Sami Pekkola
S.P.C. Arnold
Royce Calverley
Ross Weaver
Ronald Marsh
Roland Cooper
Rodger Cooley
Robert Sulentic
Robert Mauler
Robert Fisher
Richard Parker
Richard McNutt
Ricardo Macedo -
   GEMAC Porto
Rhel ná DecVandé
Rebecca Glass
Ray Gleeson
Randy Holte
Rallane Lafarell
Petri Kosonen
Peter Petermann
Paul Williams
Paul Tevis
Patrik Olterman
Patrick Leonard
Patrick Fessler
Oula Kitti
Otto Kopra
Nuutti Vertanen
Noora Kumpulainen
Nikodemus Siivola
Nico Möller
Nick Wright
Nick Sycks
Nathan Black
N.C. Monahans
Mirja Kuronen
Mira Aaltio

Mikko Sillanpää
Mikko Parviainen
Mikko Mustajärvi
Mikko Korhonen
Mikko Hänninen
Mike OBrien
Michael Troop
Michael Sims
Michael Kennedy
Michael Jarvis
Michael Horgen
Matthew Stewart-Fulton
Matthew Roche
Matthew Lewis
Matthew Benedict
Matt Howe
Mat Abel
Martin Taves
Markku Rontu
Mark Jolliff
Mark Davidson
Mark Carrol
Mark Bottomley
Mark Birchall
Marcus Taylor
Magi Hernandez
Mackenzie Cosens
Maciej Baranski
Maarten Bazuin
Lorenzo Marchese
Lonin League
Lloyd Eldred
leev2727
Lee Marshall
L'Arte Della Bellica
Lars Fock
Kristin Dahlström
Kristian Guivarra
Kris Corah
Konstantin Tsvetkov

182

Kliment Yanev
Kit Smith
Kevin Purtell
Kevin O'Brien
kendrik
Ken Mayfield
Keith Nelson
Keegan Blunk
Katherine Fanning
Kai Crystalla
Juuso Koivunen
Justin Weaver
Justin Snyder
Justin Masters
Jussi Hytönen
Jussi Hattara
Juliean Galak
Jouni Alanärä
Josias Arcadia
Joshua Gilbrech
Jorge Araujo
Jordan Hinckley
Joni Karjalainen
John Rechtoris
John Porter
John McClaughlin
John Linzy
Johanus Haidner
Joe Loder
Jocelyn Thiery
Jeremy Tavan
Jeremy Bornstein
Jeff Larson
Javier Chamorro Bernal
Jason Daub
Jarno Klok
Jarkko Hietaniemi
Janne Hurskainen
Jan Kukkamäki
James McCracken
J Landels
Isto Sipilä
Ilpo Luhtala
Ian Mowat
Hubert Chaumette
horsebows
Hildo Biersma
Heikki Hallamaa

Haden Parkes
Gruss Pierre-Marie
Gregory Poulos
Gregorio Manzanera
Greg Henrikson
Gordon Passmore
Glenn Adrian
Gindi Wauchope
George C Lewis
Gav Fuller
Gary G. & Margaret
   Hernandez
Garrett Harper
Franklin Walther
Francesco Maisto
Florian Cesic
Erwan Bineau
Ernesto Maldonado
Erica Stark
Eric Mauer
Eric Artzt
Emil Lindfors
Emanuele Triches
Ellery von Dassow
Edward W. Sleight, Jr.
Dylan Knowles
Drew Lackovic
Dr. Kuowei Chiu
Dr. Greg Hicks
Dominic Robertson
Diniz F. Cabreira
Dawfydd Kelly
David W Glaeser
David M. Monahan
David Long
Dave Wayne
Daniel Marsh
Daniel Cadenbach
Dallas Burnworth
Curtis Fee
Culann Farrell
Craig Gunderson
Corrado Roggeri
Colin Deady
Christopher Halpin
Christopher Blakey
Christian Punga-
   Kronberg

Christian Fleischhacker
Christian Engelund
Chris Myers
Chris Kinsella
Chris Cooke
Charles Deily
Cecilia Äijälä
Cay Blomqvist
Carey Martell
Britton Cooke
Brian Stewart
Brian Hart
Brian Ferguson
Brian Batronis
Benjamin Ford
Benjamin Cassart
Bence Benedek
Ben Thomas
Bastian Busch-Garbe
Bas Croezen
Bart Kapteijns
Baptiste Bouvret
Arttu Junnila
Artis Aboltins
Arnim Sommer
Anthony Hurst
Anthony Debot
Andy Gibson
Andrew South
Andrew Sefton
Andrew Rozycki
Andrew Moore
Andrew Mizener
Andrew Malloy
Andreas Narits
Anders Malmsten
Alwin Klick
Alexandre Gilbert
Alexander Sushko
Alexander Hollinger
Alex Ripa
Alex P. Wirtz
Aleksi Airaksinen
Alec Plumb
Alberto Dainese
Akihiro Idewaki
Aidan Blake

ACKNOWLEDGEMENTS

I started learning Forms back in the eighties when I took up karate at the age of about eight. It has been part of my training ever since. The idea of teaching Form application by application, and making sure every action in the Form has a reason to be there (and one which is understood by the student), came from the way I was taught T'ai Chi Chuan in the early nineties, by Steve Fox. The way Steve insisted that we understood what every movement was for, and why we do it a certain way in the Form, has been the base upon which I have built all of my Form development and teaching.

The content of this book has been developed sword-in-hand with the help of many of my students and colleagues. The specific drills in this book have been especially influenced by Joni Karjalainen, Jouni Alanärä, Ilpo Luhtala, Henry Vilhunen, Eric Artzt, Zoë Chandler and Janne Högdahl. The willingness of my students to tell me they disagree and then point to the page in Fiore where they think I've misread has been absolutely crucial to the development of my understanding of this Art. Likewise, their willingness to point out when a drill is not having the effect it's supposed to has been the driving force behind the development of the syllabus.

Abroad, thanks are especially due to my colleagues and friends Tom Leoni, Greg Mele, Sean Hayes, Scott Nimmo and Paul Wagner, many of whom have provided the opportunity to test my theories on their own students.

Jari Juslin has taken the photos for every volume so far of the *Mastering the Art of Arms* series, which is a work of love, patience and skill. On this photoshoot, he was most ably assisted by Petteri Kihlberg.

The models Satu Niemi, Janne Högdahl, Noora Kumpulainen, Mikko Behm, Ville Siivola, Henry Vilhunen, Zoë Chandler, Ilpo Luhtala, Jan Kukkamäki and Petteri Kihlberg all put up with the endless fiddling about on the photoshoot, and they have put their years of practice at the service of the wider sword community. I couldn't do this without them.

If you find this book clean, clear, and comprehensible, then the credit should go to my outstanding editor, Becca Judd, and my layout Queen, Bek Pickard. I would no more think of publishing a book without them than I would think of leaving the house without my trousers.

Writing a book takes its toll on the whole family, so let me acknowledge here the forgiving natures of my wife Michaela and daughters Grace and Katriina.

To all of the above, many thanks!

About the Author

Guy Windsor has been researching historical Italian swordsmanship and knightly combat since the late nineties, and he has been teaching the Art of Arms professionally since 2001. His books include *The Swordsman's Companion*, *The Duellist's Companion*, *Veni Vadi Vici*, and the *Mastering the Art of Arms* series. In 2012 he co-created the swordfighting card game, *Audatia*. He also blogs on swordsmanship and other matters at guywindsor.net/blog .

He lives in Helsinki, Finland, with his wife and daughters.

www.swordschool.com
www.guywindsor.com
www.audatiagame.com

CPSIA information can be obtained
at www.ICGtesting.com
Printed in the USA
BVHW041342070719
552774BV00002B/128/P

9 789527 157060